Solitaire

*the text of this book is printed
on 100% recycled paper*

A narrative by

Aimee Liu

Solitaire

HARPER COLOPHON BOOKS
Harper & Row, Publishers
New York, Cambridge, Hagerstown, Philadelphia, San Francisco
London, Mexico City, São Paulo, Sydney

To my family

A hardcover edition of this book is published by Harper & Row, Publishers.

SOLITAIRE. Copyright © 1979 by Aimee Liu. All rights reserved. Printed in the United States of America. No part of this book may be used or reproduced in any manner whatsoever without written permission except in the case of brief quotations embodied in critical articles and reviews. For information address Harper & Row, Publishers, Inc., 10 East 53rd Street, New York, N.Y. 10022. Published simultaneously in Canada by Fitzhenry & Whiteside Limited, Toronto.

First HARPER COLOPHON edition published 1980.

ISBN: 0-06-090767-3

80 81 82 83 84   10 9 8 7 6 5 4 3 2 1

Contents

Foreword

THE CHILD I was baby-sitting lay asleep upstairs. His parents weren't due home for another three hours, ample time for temptation to seize me. The lure of the television, the call of my homework were no competition for the magnet of the kitchen: food. Like a creature obsessed, neither tasting nor thinking, I burrowed through cupboards, refrigerator, cookie jar, and freezer. Grabbing fistfuls of Mallomars and brownies, gulping ice cream, Jell-O, and cheese, I was indiscriminate in my gorging. Frenzied, as though possessed by some malevolent phantom, I raced through the larder and could quit only after collapsing in glutted agony. Then, when the spell finally broke, I loathed myself for such weakness and raged at my failure of willpower.

Staggering to the bathroom, I presented myself for penitence. The mirror mercilessly cast its wrath upon me. My reflection resembled that of a bloat-bellied malnutrition victim. I weighed under 90 pounds. My scrawny arms, bony chest, and spindly legs cried out in protest against the distended abdomen of my cruel binge. The sight nauseated me. No doubt about it, eating was evil. My faith in the virtue of abstinence grew the longer I stood examining myself. It sent me into spasms of remorse over my greed and propelled me into a program of redemption.

I began by vomiting. Like yoga, my method relied on muscle contraction and concentrated control. But unable to purge myself completely this way, I worked out a backup maneuver. My magic cure was Ex-Lax, taken at three times the recommended dosage. It was like swallowing Drano. The only problem was that the effects were not instantaneous, and I was desperate for immediate relief. I could feel the calories turning to fat as I waited. My last resort was exercise. Like an expectant mother, I bent over my swollen stomach to touch toes, gasped through hundreds of jumping jacks, and struggled through feverish sit-ups. Not even the impending homecoming of my employers could subdue me. Keeping an ear cocked for the sound of the garage door opening, I kept working out for as long as possible. I was haunted by the thought that a single carbohydrate might escape my frenzy and become flesh.

My penance lasted days afterward. Rejecting all but the merest tastes of food, I raged at my parents as they urged me to eat. My mother worried. My father winced at the sight of my protruding clavicles. But I kept examining the fluctuations of the bathroom scale with the zeal of a religious fanatic. When, at the end of a three- or four-day fast, my pelvis sank to a hollow shell once again, I gloried in this proof of strength and determination. Loss of weight had become my personal path to honor; starvation was the goal of my adolescence.

Chapter One

Backward Glances

MINE WAS A CHILDHOOD frosted with affluence, filled with adventure, and sprinkled generously with loving care. Throughout the early years I led a cupcake existence, wrapped in my parents' unspoken promises that they had me destined for the best of all possible worlds. They would treat me to experiences out of the ordinary and nourish me on the good fortune of their success. They would educate me, groom me in keeping with their impeccable taste, and then, one day, would release me to take the reins on my own. But first they would make sure that I appreciated the special kind of wealth to which I'd been born and which I would have to live up to.

My earliest recollections date back to the two years my family spent in India. I was just three when we moved there. Scott, my brother, was eleven. My father spent the better part of those years winging about the Orient as he searched out films for the United Nations Documentary Film Department, and my mother spent her days organizing the Emporium, an

1

Indian design center for handicrafts and hand-loomed fabric. But neither Scott nor I felt any sense of neglect. We attended school with our international compatriots—the children of State Department representatives, of Ford Foundation workers, and of delegates of other assorted global agencies. It was, as I look back on it, an idyllic life for a child.

We lived in the diplomatic enclave in a house that shimmered under the care of a small host of servants. As per the norm for Westerners residing in Delhi, we employed a cook, gardener, sweeper, bearer, and a sequence of ayahs to look after my brother and me. In addition to the members of our own household, however, we had at our disposal an overwhelming array of neighborhood playmates, their servants, and a constant, astonishing native street parade of passing bullocks, bicycles, tongas, and pedestrians. The sights were both thrilling and alarming. There were sometimes elephants with bells on their tails, but I also saw starving babies peppered with flies and wraithlike ancients plodding miles to do work for pennies. We visited emerald gardens watered by shooting fountains and punctuated by scarlet, ivory, and golden blossoms, but we also shopped in Old Delhi, where skeletal beggars pawed at our sleeves. There were snake charmers and sadhus, temples to rats and monkeys, and thousands sleeping in the streets, but to me it was all an integral part of the mystical, outrageous place I called home. Too young to worry at the suffering and too naive to ignore it, I accepted it as an unavoidable part of life in this crazy world. Healthy, safe, and happy myself, I watched the contrasts weave through the streets and took great pleasure in the exhilaration of constant surprise. Not for many years would the paradoxes come back to haunt me. In the meantime I felt spiritually at ease, as perhaps only a child can.

India glistens in my memory like a brocaded tapestry of color, sound, and scents. We take trips into the mountains where Kashmiri houseboats float on water-lilied lakes and Kiplingesque hill stations overlook citrine valleys. Bejeweled temples glitter with thousands of candles during the nights of Diwali, the festival of light; and during Holi, the celebration of fertility, the streets blaze gaudily with explosions of colored water. The climatic changes are just as startling as the cultural displays. One night the air feels balmy and sweet, the next it turns to poison. Sometimes storms leap, like the cyclone in *The Wizard of Oz*, out of nowhere. In summer we sleep on the roof, our beds crude charpoys. These cots are wood frames strung with hemp rope. They are uncomfortable, but the sky twinkles with diamond stars and the darkness smells of flowers, and I don't mind that it's hard to sleep. But then the winds begin to churn. The dust storm is coming. My parents yell for us to go downstairs. They grab bedding and slam doors and windows as we descend. For days the choking attack may last. It fills the house with veils of dirt, despite all attempts at insulation, and whirls across the desert city like a mad hatter. And while my mother despairs of the filth and worries over the fate of the homeless poor, I thrill to the excitement with a three-year-old's careless delight. Danger and despair are foreign to me. I stand laughing with my back to a splintery window jamb. My brother plays tag with me this afternoon while my parents are off at a tea party. Taunting me from across the room, he can't see the scorpion on the ledge behind me. He goads me toward the window where the deadly villain tickles my fingertip. I think the itch is a bit of screening come loose from the frame, but as the irritation continues I look down and scream. It's horribly ugly, but dangerous? The thought never occurs to me. In fact, I'm pleased to discover that my life was in danger. It makes me feel special that I've been so spared. I must have an important future ahead of me.

Each home in the diplomatic enclave is surrounded by a high wall of mortar and clay. The grounds inside these fortress walls seem like fairytale gardens designed for small children at play. Cut off from the native bustle and stilled by the beat of the desert sun, they flourish under the care of full-time gardeners. They become, with a quick wish, jungles of Africa or tropical rainforests. Alone at play beneath the shrubs that border our yard, I hunt wild game. The earth under my knees feels moist. It glows with the reflected daylight, slightly green through the leaves. I push confidently through the tropical petals and vines, stalking the predatory beasts whose eyes blaze at me from behind the trunks of imaginary trees. Beyond the sheltering vegetation the day swelters and glares, but deep within my fantasy woodland I feel only the heat of the hunt. When suddenly I meet my prey, however, he defies me to harm him. I can't. He is a determined little fellow the size of my fist, his shell a perfect spiral the hue of sand. We share an immunity to danger. I respect his intrepid determination and sense of direction. We become instant friends, this fearless traveler and I, and though we won't ever meet again, I will always consider him a symbol of freedom and bliss.

It is October 1958 when we return to Glenridge, Connecticut. We drive from the docks of New York in a green Mercedes that my parents bought in Germany on the way home. Home? I balk at the word now. As far as I'm concerned we've left my home. As we speed along concrete byways past franchised supermarkets and barren shopping centers, I recognize nothing of America and like little of what I see. I refuse to pledge allegiance to the flag of the United States. . . .

We turn up a drive between evergreen shrubs and steep glacial rock formations, round the top of the hill, and slip into the somber pocket of land where my parents tell me we live.

The neighbors have planted a multicolored sign at the fork in the road, lest we have lost direction after two years away. Cheery balloons fly from the post, and a painted clown laughs and points out our way. (Is this a homecoming or a birthday party?) But despite the merry guidepost, this place feels eerie, too quiet and empty. Where are the children, the animals, the beggars, the sounds? I miss the drumbeat, the tempo of my former life. Here there's not a soul in sight, only the crimson leaves of autumn falling to greet us.

The house in which I will spend the rest of my childhood looms handsomely before us. The antithesis of our white-washed, Delhi domicile, this sprawling lodge boasts fieldstone, cyprus wood, and glass. My parents view it proudly. They built it themselves before I was born. My brother leaps from the car and runs to explore. He remembers the way the living room snuggles into the crook of an abandoned rock quarry. He has played for hours in the graveled patio out back, splashed in the fountained goldfish pond, and hidden in the crannies of my mother's rock garden. I recall none of it. Following my mother through the cathedrallike living room, I feel a dwarf and an outsider. Slate floors, windows twenty feet high, great beamed ceilings, and everywhere the aura of forest (real this time, not make-believe)—I don't know what to make of it.

At the front we have pasture, on the sides woods, and at the back sweeping lawns and gardens. But unlike the yards of India, ours here has a wild look about it. Not manicured by gardeners, not fertilized and pampered, these grounds seem almost self-sufficient. I listen for the chant of bear and monkey wallahs, for the pipe song of snake charmers and the rasp of sweepers' brooms. But the only sound is the chilly moan of breezes among the pines. This place promises loneliness and an inexplicable sort of gloom.

My father takes me for a tour of the neighborhood and tells me its story. I try, for future reference and to establish a sense of belonging, to get the details straight. The marble amphitheater (facsimile of a Greek arena), hidden in the back woods, was built in the spirit of bygone eras. Sparkling white and flanked by a ring of overgrown Christmas trees, it is a freak product of the Great Depression. Its creator was one of the fortunate few who could afford to be generous during hard times. An architect unscathed by the crash, he designed a house for a client in Vermont who paid him in marble instead of dollars. The ingenious Mr. Blanchard had his prize brought in trainloads to Connecticut, drew up plans for his personal stage, and set the hungry laborers of the area to work. At about the same time he had built for his children two clay-floored tennis courts and a fifty-foot swimming pool, which resembles a Polynesian watering hole. It is fashioned into a bed of natural rock and fitted with a circulation system that works by means of waterfalls. A sand-filled sunbathing area lines one side, a tiered rock garden the other. I imagine it filled with laughing children diving inexhaustibly into water that shimmers in the sunshine. I pretend that we can hear the chatter of grown-ups as they volley in the courts across the way. For now the courts are empty, overgrown with goldenrod, and frogs leap in the stagnant puddle of water that still remains in the bottom of the pool. The owner, a retired actress, doesn't care to entertain any longer. My father tells me that in the old days, before I was born, there were grand parties here. All the neighbors gathered for barbecues. They hung paper lanterns in the trees and floated watermelons in the pool to chill. That was when my brother was my age, and the other kids of the community had not yet gone away to boarding school and college. Why did I miss out on all the fun? Why is there no one my age here now to keep me company? I feel cheated and alone.

All the splendors of field and stream can't comfort me. We visit a secret pond over the hill behind our front pasture. Water lilies float on its surface. Skunk cabbage flourish on its shore. We sight a muskrat scurrying for cover in the woods and tiptoe across the dam that drains this man-made lake. Then my father shows me an island which I may take for my very own. It rises out of a bog on the edge of our property and has a carpet of moss all over it. Its only resident is a single baby oak tree and an imbedded rock, the ideal seat for me. I plan to play explorer here, to build bridges around it and, after winter snows, to shovel roads across the surface of the bog and make towns in miniature on the ice. But I don't want to realize these plans all by myself. As my father proudly assesses his estate I try to echo his delight at coming home, but the annoying nudge of loneliness spoils my best intentions.

On the Monday of our second week back in the States my mother takes me to school. North Mianus has been in session for over a month already. I feel like an interloper, walking into classes in progress. My mother and Miss Bloom, the kindergarten teacher, pore over my registration papers while I survey the situation from a corner by the door.

I am different from the other children in the room. I am one-quarter Chinese. I have lived in the Orient. I have sailed across the ocean and flown in planes. I have applauded dancing bears, taken a seat in Nehru's lap, and cast marigolds on Gandhi's tomb. But the little girls I see playing store by the opposite wall think all Indians wear feathers in their hair. Their world stops at the edge of Candlewood Park, and their notion of a great excursion is a trip to New York City. Everyone here has fair skin and a well-nourished air. The scene before me looks like an advertisement for Sealtest milk, quite a contrast to the variegated environment I have left behind. Whether my difference marks me superior or inferior worries me. I feel both at the same time and wish I felt neither. But the fact remains: The homogeneity of these kindergarteners excludes me. I feel as though I've just unwillingly dropped in from another planet.

Then my mother leaves. The panic that results is like nothing I've ever known before. Stranded, I view this antiseptic playroom world with mistrustful eyes. Miss Bloom acts friendly enough, but the little people threaten me. Tina, Kimmy, Wendy, Cappy, Susan, Peter, Connie, Kenny, Sam, Billy, Stan—the names wash over me at random, all too American. I am used to mingled nationalities and strange-sounding titles. It's fun to roll the vowels and consonants of exotic languages across one's tongue. When everyone's a stranger, struggling with communication barriers, everyone somehow belongs. Here, where all the names sound flatly alike, any deviation from the norm strikes out. A-I-M-E-E, I spell, L-I-U. The other kids look at me as though I'm crazy. I try to explain, my first name is French. My last is Chinese. But they can't, or won't, understand, and the teacher interrupts to tell us it's time for cookies and milk.

Not hungry, I eat. It's a constant game of follow-the-leader, this kindergarten business, and it bores me. We must bring blankets from home, spread them out on the floor and, in the middle of the day, pretend to sleep. The drawn shades and doused lights can't fool me. I am not used to naps, don't like to rest, but because I am obedient, I close my eyes and stretch out, stiff as a twig, until Miss Bloom allows us to rise. It makes no sense, but I comply, just as I make believe that I like to play house, skip rope, and construct skyscrapers out of blocks. When my mother picks me up at the end of the day I wail of frustration and boredom. Still, another side of me longs to fit in.

A strange new craving for companionship overwhelms me, but it is thwarted from the start by circumstance. If my family lived in Candlewood Park or on Primrose Drive or Mimosa Lane, my problems would be solved. I could learn to like the other kids if I lived around them, played with them after school, cruised with them on weekends from backyard to backyard. They would include me in their plans and learn that I am not weird after all. They would have me over for dinner, and afterward I could join too when the neighborhood youngsters came out to play softball in the street. During the winter we would all sled together, and skate on the Mianus River. We would trade boyfriends and best friends, the girls down the block and I, and give each other surprise birthday parties (with the help of our mothers, of course). But the only assistance my mother is able to give me is to drive me over to visit those paradise neighborhoods. And no matter how frequently I come to play, no matter how familiar my face becomes in the community "gangs," we all know that I remain an outsider.

It isn't only physical distance that separates me from them. Our life-styles, our parents, our habits too have little in common. My home is a world unto itself, my family unlike any other I meet in Glenridge. Ozzie-and-Harriet patterns really do predominate in the suburbs, but not at our house. While my schoolmates' parents meet for bridge games and backyard barbecues, mine attend receptions at the French Embassy, balls at the Waldorf, and openings at the Metropolitan. And, to the stupefaction of the Candlewood Park crowd, they frequently take me with them to these functions. At penthouse dinner parties I steal the show. That I am the only seven-year-old among ambassadors and presidents never bothers me. I strut like Shirley Temple through the reception lines and chat freely with foreign ministers until my bedtime, when I trundle off to some darkened bedroom to doze between mountains of coats and furs until my parents are ready to leave. There are recitals of African music in the nave of the General Assembly, sessions of the Ecumenical Council, and luncheons at the home of the Secretary-General. I cultivate a taste for caviar, brie, and strawberries in wine, and learn to address adults by their first names. The world of the elite, a fantasy land far from my daily woes, delights me. The scent of protocol tempts me to grow up, or at least pretend to grow up, very fast.

Thanksgiving 1960. It's the year the Jones boys slather their pumpkin pie with ketchup while our parents argue over chestnut dressing and creamed onions about the future of JFK. It's the year my brother and Chas Jones, both fifteen, remain downstairs after dinner and sip brandy with the grown-ups while Cliff Jones and his buddy, Dick, take me up to the attic and rape me. Aged twelve, they laugh. Aged seven, I don't.

Of course, I don't really consider it a big deal. Not necessarily a bad deal, anyhow. I believe what they tell me: It's just fooling around; it's my privilege to be included in their games. One little girl with two big boys, I am their obedient slave, anxious to please as long as they'll let me stay. Oh, please, please like me! Please accept me! Show that you want me, that you approve of me. I'll do anything to be included, to prove that I'm good enough to belong. Let me into your club too!

We play tag around the attic first. Catching splinters in our socks and cobwebs in our hair, we sing about Casey Jones and choo-choo-choo through dark, musty closets.

Downstairs the adults chortle at some innocent joke, their mirth rising through the floorboards in muted waves of heedless satiety. While they lean back and rest after the feast, my youthful hosts work off the meal in other ways. I blush at the thought that my parents think we're watching TV. There's something naughty afoot up here. Whatever Cliff has in mind, I sense it's forbidden.

"I know! Let's take off all our clothes and play horse!"

Dick eagerly seconds the motion. I keep quiet. What's so great about going naked? You can play horse with your clothes on just as well. I have never seen a boy in the raw, never particularly wanted to. But what has a pawn to say against a king's wishes?

We strip and play horse. They ride me bareback on their shoulders. They toss me back and forth between them, all the while hushing my nervous shrieks. Cliff scampers down to make sure the door at the bottom of the stairs is locked against detection from below. Suddenly I'm frightened. Why are they so worried, so afraid of being found out? Security fades. I am out of control, damned if I do and damned if I don't. But do or don't what? Bewildered and masking my terror, I must simply wait and see what they have in store for me.

"Now let's switch places," Cliff whispers loudly, leering. They giggle together, sharing a secret they know I don't know. They carry me to a corner under the eaves. Cliff lies on his back, knees bent, and stretches his arms upward to receive me. Dick lifts me over him and guides my movements from behind. I straddle this peculiar body. Crouch, kneel, stroke, stroke. Our skins stick. It tickles and embarrasses me. This is pointless, not fun at all. Even the boys have stopped laughing. Their genitals disgust me. So ugly, hanging loose and limp, what function can they possibly serve? The shriveled sacs of flesh graze my under-aged chest and belly, explore between my thighs. And then a quick, awkward jab of pain as the sword enters me, numbs me. Dick stares, wide-eyed but not horrified, so I must not be bleeding. Has he wounded me then? I laugh and cry, and wonder why. Not talking, the boys roll me between them like a larger-than-life baby doll to fondle and tweak and manipulate as they please. Cliff tickles me to keep me smiling. I dare not scream or struggle, though I long to pull loose and run downstairs to my mother's arms and the rosy glow of parlor talk. They maul me, caress me clumsily, and explore me like a foreign animal. It's hard to believe that these are signs of affection.

At last the time is up. My father calls that I am going home. The boys swear me to secrecy as we quickly dress. They have honored me with their trust. I must not betray them. But they don't need to worry about any oaths of secrecy. Whatever it is that we've done wrong, I accept the blame myself. It was an adventure, one to which I agreed, even encouraged. As long as they let me stay in their club I'll keep their secret and, if need be, take the rap. Deep inside I hate the boys for what they've done, but I turn the accusation for their mysterious sin against myself instead of them.

It fell like a shaft out of midnight. My forehead burst into blood as my head reeled with a thousand sparks. Swathed in a twirl of curtains and sheets, I tumbled back onto my mother's bed while outside the dog howled. In an instant my mother swept me into her arms and raced me to the bathroom to cleanse my messy but minor wounds. My father never woke through it all.

Earlier in the evening dangerous visions had danced through my head. I met again the rattlesnake my parents had taken me to view at a local museum that afternoon. Entrancing me as none of the cobras in India had, this hideous creature coiled in his cage warned me of imminent doom. He was my enemy. He would not let me escape. At bedtime I had trouble falling asleep, though curled in my tightest fetal position, and hugged myself for comfort. But when finally taken to dream, I felt his threat in its purest essence. My assassin slipped from his mountaintop prison, slithered down Putnam Avenue, and sped by the light of the moon straight toward my bedroom. He knew the way intuitively and arrived outside my window just as I woke screaming.

My mother called sleepily from her room for me to join her in bed. I was too scared to move. But then, the silence and darkness were worse. My mother had fallen back to sleep and I was once more alone. Whether I closed my eyes or kept them open, my attacker still threatened to appear. Be brave. He's imaginary, remember. Take a deep breath and plunge. But sometimes demons of fantasy can be realer than real. Gasping for strength, I leapt from my covers across the room, scooted out into the hall and around the corner to the safety of my mother's sleeping form.

So soft, so rounded, tousled in long Grecian nightgown folds, she received me without words. Her waist-length hair, unfamiliarly released from its daytime French twist, enfolded me. She kissed my forehead in somnolent welcome and pulled her cashmere blanket up under my chin. A stranger to this world of parental repose, I nestled into her scent of perfume and night flesh, and, for a moment, forgot my fears.

But within minutes Clem began to bark outside. Perhaps he

had sniffed the snake? My father mumbled in his sleep. My mother tossed in annoyance and flicked me out of bed to let Clem in. The carpet felt cold and crawly beneath my feet. I tripped over the drapes that cloaked the door and, without pulling them back, began to fumble with the lock. Clem again cried in the darkness. He sounded as terrified as I. I yanked at the knob and the door flew open. The curtain rod came crashing down, enveloping me in shrouds of blood-drenched fabric. The dog yelped, my mother sprang into action, and my father continued to doze in peace.

He is a silent character, my father, forty years my senior and inscrutably intelligent. He works hard, rushing into New York early each morning and returning late at night, and rarely speaks to me. His is a world of politics and international affairs. He has no time for my child's concerns. Not cold or cruel or strict, he wears a carapace of quiet that prohibits intrusion. He needn't withdraw if approached or beckoned; he simply doesn't respond. But I doubt he means to offend me. Certainly he loves and provides for me generously enough. If only we could talk.

During my vacations from school I commute with him to New York to spend whole days at the United Nations. We sit like strangers on the train, he chain-smoking and scanning the morning paper, I trying to think of something to say. That my teacher has praised my penmanship? That my third grade was going to take a field trip to the beach to hunt for horseshoe crabs? That Kimmy has invited me to her birthday party? I can think of nothing that would interest him, and so keep my mouth shut and stare. I can't believe that we look alike. He has heavy pouches beneath his eyes, and flat lids above them. As a result he seems to squint perpetually. My own eyes look like round almonds. His hair lies thick and black, beginning to glimmer gray. He keeps it trim and parted on the side. Mine hangs long and brown with flecks of auburn. Dad has a high rectangular forehead, a prominent nose, and incipient jowls. My face is round, capped with a widow's peak, and my nose is almost comically small. Why does it bother me that we have so little in common?

At the end of our ride the myriad world of the city distracts me. Mammoth and hushed as a cathedral, Grand Central is awesome. On the distant ceiling an ancient astrological chart describes the heavens in gold and green. So sedate it seems by contrast with the garish Kodak photographs and fluorescent coffee shops. I find something comforting in the way this great station spans time and taste and distance. There seems room here for every age and nationality, rich and poor alike. But my father has no time for rumination. I skip to keep up with him as he strides to work. He walks briskly, never stopping to gaze in shop windows, and I have a hard time catching all the sights and sounds of rush hour. A tall clown dressed in polka dots and floppy shoes hands out free doughnuts as promotion for a new savings bank on 42d Street. A businessman who smells of bacon and eggs brushes me as he passes and knocks my straw hat off. The blind Viking, Moondog, sings his songs outside the U.S. Post Office, and across the street a tattered bag lady pleads for spare change. Why are some people fed so well and others not at all? What makes us so lucky and them so poor? My father pushes on, not answering. He's in a hurry to get to work. He's chief of the Visitor's Bureau, and it's his job to brief the tour guides every morning.

Across the outdoor plaza we race, through the revolving doors, and into the great hall of the General Assembly Building. The suspended model of the Sputnik was a gift from the

Soviet Union, the wall of nickel-plated windows from Canada. By my eighth birthday I know most of the tour by heart, but I never tire of coming here. In my father's basement office we separate. He leaves me to the care of secretaries and guides, and spins into his official day. Perhaps we will meet for lunch in the Delegate's Dining Room or the Press Club in the Secretariat, but most likely we won't see each other again until it's time to go home. The women in the office don't mind. They ooh and aah over this sweet little tike in smocked dress and patent leather shoes, the boss's daughter come to spend a day playing international affairs. As for me, there's more than enough to keep me entertained, never mind my father's laissez-faire attitude. The guides whisk me like a VIP through security and down labyrinthine corridors closed to the general public. I sit in on meetings of ECOSOC and the Trusteeship Council, and listen to debates about nuclear warfare in the Security Council. Utter strangers marvel at me. They think I'm terribly precocious. I do my best to act the part, and when my father greets me at the end of the day I make sure he gets a fine report on my conduct. He acts proud at that, and boasts that I will one day bloom as a lady ambassador.

But the cosmopolitan light in my eye fades quickly with return to Glenridge. In the confines of my own home I can't fake precocity. At dinner I politely remain at table long after finishing my meal and listen as my parents dissect the state of the nation and world. They wage nightly warfare over political points of view and the meaning of presidential appointments. They fight with such intensity that I, ignorant of the issues, hear hatred in their voices and believe each such meal to be their last together.

Things may start off peacefully. My brother and I help my Mother set the table while Dad drinks a whiskey and soda and plods on through the newspaper (a never-ending occupation). Scott tickles me, sends me writhing helpless into gales of laughter, until my mother sternly commands him to stop and slice the bread for supper. The three of us chatter about the day's activities and make plans for the morrow, and when the meal is ready my father joins us.

Things quiet down as Dad carves the meat and apportions the vegetables. He tells my mother that Haile Selassie today addressed the General Assembly. There's trouble with the mercenaries fighting in the Congo. The border disputes continue in the Middle East. Viet Nam looks bleaker by the day. Gulping forkfuls of rice pilaf, I swim through the conversation like a minnow in a stream of wine. It makes me feel giddy, all this talk above my head, but also slightly ill at ease. Is there nothing here for me to latch onto, nothing that I can understand? I want to participate, or at least to learn, but the issues and answers flow faster and faster, leaving me far behind. My mother, an idealistic liberal, cries for the abolition of colonialism and defends nonviolent protest. She heatedly condemns the South African government's apartheid system and launches into sweeping comparisons of despotic regimes around the world. The more she talks the louder and faster and more insistent she becomes. Dad, who discourages such extrapolation, closes up again when Mom begins to speak. You can see by the way he eats that she annoys him. He attacks his meal not with relish or gusto, but with a predatory greed. He macerates his potato, green beans, and squash, and drowns them in thick brown gravy. He fastidiously picks the meat from bones, even taking them in his fingers and gnawing them clean. And when the food is finished he pulls a large hunk of bread across his plate to sop up any remains. The more elaborate Mom's rant, the more fiercely Dad eats. He never interrupts, but he keeps time with her fury through the tempo of his knife and fork. Only at the end of her tirade, and when he has sated himself, will he comment on her theories. Almost always he finds fault with them. She accuses him of criticizing her intelligence. He hurls facts and figures at her to substantiate his claims. She damns his photographic memory and screams for imagination. He calmly informs her that she is wrong, that no theory can succeed without accurate information to back it up, and that she inevitably forms opinions without knowing the facts. And so the seesaw snaps. Mom thunders off to the back of the house, slamming doors and breaking dishes as she goes. Dad takes wordless refuge in his study, where he pores over piles of tax forms and bills. Scott drifts to the living room to watch *Palladin*, and I stumble off to my room to cry.

Why can't I be like my brother, aloof and perpetually amused by Mom and Dad's disputes? He doesn't feel threatened by them. Nor does he feel excluded. At fifteen, he takes nothing very seriously except BB guns and cars. I wish I were as independent as he. But the combination of my mother's temper and my father's impassivity crushes me. At least if I understood what they were fighting about I could choose sides and participate and it would not be so bad. But I feel as though I'm on the other side of a glass wall, a one-way mirror. I can see my parents, and through a loudspeaker their voices reach me, but I cannot get through to them how I feel about their monstrous fights, cannot inform them that they're hurting me. And they, insensitive to my reactions, refuse to look my way.

For, in some curious way that I can't detect, the mealtime matches bind my parents together. Whether for energy release or emotional stimulation, they need to cross swords. Frequently. And they don't restrict themselves to dueling over foreign affairs. Domestic matters also feed the flames of contention. It's still a battle of facts and figures against principle and reason, only the fuel for the fight consists of personal idiosyncrasies instead of international diplomacy. There was, for example, the Great Lumber Controversy. . . .

The figures Dad was defending in this case were bargain prices. He had found, at a back-country garage sale, six hand-hewn cherrywood beams. Each one was about sixty inches in circumference, and twelve feet long. What he would do with them mattered not; at ten dollars apiece, my father considered them a bargain. He had to have them. It was not surprising, given my father's passion for junk. He, of course, would never refer to his trophies as junk. No, they are rare finds, incredible buys, and the hunt for them is his favorite hobby. He spends whole Saturdays, classified ads in hand, prowling thrift shops and commission marts, tag sales and discount houses. He haunts rummage rooms, auction warehouses, and liquidated estates, and returns laden at the end of the day with extravagant gifts for everyone. Most bear labels or insignia of class— Tiffany asparagus servers, irreparable Cartier watches, Mark Cross desk accessories with the monograms of deceased tycoons, jodhpurs from Abercrombie and Fitch with cigarette burns in the seat. His study overflows with cast-off quality. The garage bursts with malfunctioning power saws and slabs of formica, piles of discarded shelving and sheet rock, and hundreds of tools collected since his first year of marriage. Dad has never put together his workshop, but he's getting ready. So it was not at all out of character when he rented a truck, drove twenty miles to make his collection, and arrived home with sixty dollars' worth of wood of indeterminate purpose. Nevertheless, when Mom saw him coming she began to seethe like an overloaded pressure cooker.

By suppertime the storm warnings were out. Beef stroganoff was for dinner, and all afternoon the kitchen had been ringing with the noise of my mother's wrath. She makes no effort ever to conceal her temper from my brother and me, but goes about her business like a tornado oblivious to obstructions in its path. Hurling pans and clattering spoons, she voices her grievances freely without regard for the family audience. She in fact needs us there to absorb her rage and strengthen her convictions that she is right and Dad wrong. Hers is the voice of reason and pragmatism, after all. She waved her knife in gesticulation as she accused my father of wastefulness and perhaps even insanity. She threw cubes of beef in flour and sent them flying into the skillet to sizzle in butter before she mixed them with sour cream and wine. Even at her most violent my mother is an excellent cook.

Lest Scott and I creep off, leaving her to talk to herself, she assigned us both kitchen duty. I was to prepare the Pillsbury Poppin' Fresh dinner rolls for baking. Scott was to whip the cream to go on the strawberry tart for dessert. Given our choice, we'd both have preferred to evacuate the premises and forget about the meal, but Mom would stand for no such cowardice. In her black moods any hint of rebuff, from any quarter, equals high treason. Were we to back away, she would take it as a direct insult, attacking us every bit as vehemently as she did our father. So we kept our mouths shut, played kitchen servants, and waited for Dad to appear.

Such an absurd quarrel it seems in retrospect, but so intense and exhausting at the time! Mom's strident notes screamed through the house like deadly arrows. We listened to the harangue about waste and mismanagement through four courses of food. My father endured it without a word. He took second helpings of the stroganoff and noodles and four slices of

French bread slathered with butter. He was hungry after a hard day's work. But his silence only aggravated my mother's condition. She pounded on the table to command his attention, and demanded if he were deaf. At last he responded, his voice quivering a little with contained annoyance, and called her a bloody fool. At which point, the dining room blew up. Scott and I ran for shelter in our respective bedrooms. Even the dog kept out of sight. I was convinced that divorce would follow, and dessert had never been served.

But, remarkably, divorce didn't follow, and neither has it resulted from countless ensuing rows. At the sound of my parents' bedroom door crashing shut behind my mother, I crept down to the living room to view the aftermath of the holocaust and found my father sitting placidly in front of the television. Unruffled, apparently, he was munching Cracker Jacks and watching Perry Mason. More than a trifle confused, I settled down beside him. Was he friend or foe? He, unlike Mom, never called upon me to choose sides, and for that alone I liked him. He offered me some Cracker Jacks, but made no mention of the recent battle. Taking a handful of this pathetic consolation prize, I wondered if I was losing my mind. Quite likely even Mom, by morning, would deny the intensity of the evening. Scott was already out tinkering with the battered jalopy he was piecing together in the backyard. What an absurd whirligig this family rides! Why, I wonder, am I the only one incapable of taking it in stride? And how can I show them how their silly wars distress me?

We arrive at the home of my father's sister and her husband. It has been a long, grueling drive across country in the old green Mercedes. The whole family, Clem included, has been cooped up for two weeks. We have crossed the Painted

Desert, camped in Yosemite and Yellowstone, followed the Grand Canyon, and explored the Petrified Forest. By the time we reach Los Angeles we're all a bit edgy and tight. I, for one, am not at all prepared for the welcome that awaits us there.

"Dahlings! It's so lovely to have you here at last! Oh, but you simply must be worn *out!* Do come in and have a drink. Mamma is just now getting up from her nap, but she'll be down in a little while. She especially wants to meet *you*, little one!" My aunt tweaks my ear in a way that makes me cringe. A former glamour queen, she has retained her ebullient personality despite advancing years and widening girth, and she still speaks in the lah-di-dah cocktail manner that lends an air of mendacity to everything she says.

We follow her across a patio of chipped red slate, over an ivied threshold into a palace of a house which, she loquaciously explains, was built by Joan Blondell and Dick Powell in the days when they were still together. The view from this mountaintop villa is spectacular. A picture window in the living room looks out on a tapestry of California twinkle and dusk. In the valley garlands of headlights blaze their way toward Sunset Strip. They look like festoons of fireflies. I sip my ginger ale and marvel at the sight. The grown-ups relax with martinis and scotch, and volley anecdotes of family past and present.

Suddenly my aunt's voice, haughty and cloying, interrupts my reverie. My grandmother is coming. I am, for the first time, to meet the old lady who so many years ago dared marry a Chinese scholar and move to the Orient, then abandoned him for the sake of safety and moved back to America. She is now a snappy invalid and lives across the patio here in a private apartment. She rarely ventures out, but in honor of our visit, and especially to make my acquaintance, she has agreed to join us for dinner in the main house. I don't much want to meet her, really, but obedient as ever I rise when summoned.

Nine years to ninety, we face each other. She is a shriveled but willful old bird who frightens me with age. Her blue eyes clouded with cataracts, her gnarled fingers gripping the antimacassared arms of the divan, she is the matriarch enthroned before her assembled clan. The rose-colored bedjacket that my mother sent her for Christmas last year is tied at her throat with a velvet ribbon, but neither the pastel hues nor the sweet cloisonné barrettes that gently sweep back her soft white hair can make her seem anything but a raven to me.

Center stage now, little girl. Should I curtsy low and kiss her hand? Or should I hug her with fraudulent love? Too bashful for either display, I take a seat beside her and timidly say hello. She greets me coolly in a voice that scrapes like sandpaper. Her rouged lips pucker as she speaks, stretching the tissue-paper skin of her old white cheeks. She squints hard at me, fighting to see through the deathly veil that covers her eyes, and I wait to hear her verdict—praise or condemnation?

Finally she lifts her chin very high, looks directly into my face, and says, "My, you're a chubby little girl, aren't you?"

She isn't asking me, she's telling me, and, as the grande dame settles back into the depths of her throne, I fume in humiliation and surprise. This judgment has caught me completely off guard. It's the first time anyone's mentioned my size or weight. I was aware I was tall and strong for my age, but the idea of "chubby" has never crossed my mind. It's an insult, that much is clear, but valid? I just don't know. And how important is it, anyway? I can't decide, but I do resent it. This old woman whom I will never meet again has planted a monster in my mind. He's a predatory beast who will follow me home and lurk, waiting for a chance to crawl under my skin and release his venom.

Chapter Two

Puberty Blues

AT NOON, sometime after midnight, I stand atop the Eiffel Tower and peer across the continents. The day is clear, so clear that I see China in full detail. Genghis Khan's banners unfurl across the plains. Sun Yat-sen's army fatigues sassily catch the light, and radiant circles—straw peasant hats—bob through rice paddies mile after mile. I have a task to do. I step out, sink momentarily, then rally, and effortlessly rise on the breeze. Paris hushes into gray below and the demarcations of Belgium and Poland vanish behind me. My route passes just south of Finland, then over Moscow. How merry those striped rooftops look! How misleading. Skimming the edge of Siberia I search for the exiled Dostoevski. My dainty dress waves briskly at five hundred miles an hour, grips the sides of my body like wetted sheets. But I feel happy and pure at such swift altitudes. Confident and excited at the prospect of solving international crises, I sweep above the Himalayas and interrupt the storms

24

of Russia in time to watch clouds of thunder break over the Great Wall. My perspective geographically and historically has gone topsy-turvy, but that doesn't seem to matter in the giant scheme of things. I make a long wheelspin curve over the Yangtze to check the progress of a UN-appointed peacekeeping mission, then zoom lower to counsel the disputing generals. Gaily waving them into conference, I swoop to the rescue, enchanted swallow of peace come to inspire settlement. It's so easy when you apply a little kindness and love. They understand my principles, you see. They know I care. It just takes patience, honesty, and trust. In no time my mission is accomplished and I soar again. Higher and higher I fly, elated by the scent of success and the breath of power. The afternoon twinkles. Heading back toward France, I hear the temple bells chiming me a goodwill message from Bhutan. The fishermen on the Arabian Ocean are pulling in their nets at this hour and on the Afghan tundra herds of antelope come out to graze. In Greece, the walls of seaside villages sparkle with whitewash, and a nation of black-cloaked widows returns from market. It's nearly sundown as I pull to the north. I'm getting hungry, but feel happily weary after a good day's work. I sight the Tower once again and wave to my mother. She awaits me at the top. We will treat ourselves to tea, and I'll tell her the tale of my accomplishments. I'll make her proud of me.

She says we love each other very much. My mother and I. It's a topic that perplexes me. We sit together over chicken salad sandwiches and chocolate layer cake at Lord and Taylor's Bird Cage Restaurant. On the first forkful of mocha icing I recall Grammy Liu's remarks and ask if I must, to avoid becoming fat, forgo sweets. Ugly fat. My mother reassures me that I have nothing to worry about. She laughs pleasantly as I describe my dream and announce my desire to heal the world.

But it felt so real! I could feel the wind whipping my face and the soldiers actually stopped in the battlefields to watch me fly by. They quit fighting for me. Honestly.

"If only it could be that simple, darling." She sighs, stirs the steam from her coffee, which she drinks black, and shifts the weight of numerous packages off her grosgrained toes. The onus of global distress lies heavily with her, it's plain to see. Her face clouds at the mention of warfare. Her rouged cheeks tighten with concern for the "weary masses."

But I don't understand, if she cares so, what are we doing here in this candyland eatery? We fatten ourselves on dainty treats while verbally agonizing. What good does that do? Wouldn't it be better to suffer starvation in honor of the poverty-stricken, or to go out and march in protest at hunger and bombs? Here we sit, surrounded by tweed-suited house-wives and miniskirted secretaries, and we have the nerve to pretend that we are concerned, that we want to change the world. I put down my fork. The contradictions of the life my family leads bewilder me. It annoys me to think how obedient-ly I pattern myself according to my parents' example, how willingly I accept luxury and ease.

My mother knows nothing of my misgivings. She drinks an-other cup of coffee. I remain mute. She would not take kindly to my objections. No, she'd balk, confused at first, and then would flare up at me for criticizing her personal values and her talent as mother, citizen, and wife. She would explode like a firecracker at my contentions because she accepts, as I can't, the futility of idealism, and this insight pains her. For at age eleven I persist in believing that the problems of the masses can be solved, that one fine day the dove of peace will shower the world with olive branches and that all suffering will cease. With all their discussions and tears, my parents have promised me so. If the solution were impossible, so my naive reasoning goes, why waste all the energy on speculative quarrels?

Thinking harder and harder about it, yet feeling frustrated at the cowardice that prevents me from voicing my convictions, I start to hate my mother. I resent her ineffectual rages and breakdowns, and despise myself for submitting to her unwitting tyranny. In an instant the wars of the world condense to our relationship. Plays for power, struggles to communicate, misunderstanding, and the smashing of faith—the ingredients seem to me to remain the same, but it's so much harder to resolve this battle than it was on my Asian dream plains.

She baffles me, this woman who charges our meal on a small green plastic rectangle and leads me out to the realm of mannequins and glitter. Sophisticate, businesswoman, housewife, she juggles her roles so smoothly that I can never quite identify her. Too big of bone and solidly round to qualify in my mind as a great beauty, she nevertheless has exquisite style and a wonderful flair for clothes. Her chestnut hair twisted high and pinned with tortoiseshell combs, her wardrobe sedately color-coordinated and chicly tailored, she's established a system of personal values that overwhelms me. She smells of Je Reviens and L'Air du Temps and Chant d'Arômes, but stepping up to the counter to buy refills for her atomizers, she invariably mispronounces their names. I can neither understand nor forgive such a flaw in a woman who invests so much energy in perfect performance. Sometimes I adore her, sometimes I despise her, but always I'm in awe of her. To think that in order to grow up I might have to challenge her sends me into a panic. I would rather remain a model child.

Yet I desperately wish that I could be free. We have driven with my brother to Illinois to see him into his first year at college. Because he is to play on the freshman soccer team and has two weeks of practice before school starts, we have arrived earlier than most of the students, and the campus is empty. As I wander over the grassy lawns and quadrangles, it is easy to believe that I as well as Scott have come to stay. I stray from my family to inspect the classrooms and dining hall and pretend that my teens, so dreaded now, are over and that I have arrived, strong and beautiful and able to survive on my own.

We drive over to the fraternity house where the soccer players are to stay until the regular dormitories open up. Out front a couple of African students, who also are on the team, look up from their reading to study us. They squint and smile. They find us amusing. My parents find them handsome. I feel self-conscious.

Wearing a new red plaid jumper and my black Pappagallo shoes, I know that I look pretty. My legs are tanned from a summer of industrious sunbathing, and my hair, recently cut to chin length, is tied back with a narrow black velvet ribbon. I've been working at improving my appearance because, as soon as we return home, I am to begin junior high school. The look is older, more mature, and struggling under the present scrutiny, I am glad of it. Perhaps they think that it is I who am arriving.

My skirt hikes up as I clamber out of the back seat from under layers of suitcases, boxes, blankets, and clothes, and from inside the building there issues a cheer. My mother laughs and tells me to watch out, the boys have seen me. My father inscrutably smiles. Not too embarrassed to feel flattered, I straighten myself and adopt my most beguiling pose. Casually leaning against the fender I scan the windows for a sign of my admirers. No one is there. A television blares loudly inside.

"Hey, snap out of it, Sleeping Beauty! Give me a hand with these boxes, will you." My brother has no time for my reverie. Reluctantly I shoulder a load and follow him inside.

Five brawny athletes lounge around the common room. They're watching television, guzzling beer, and exchanging risqué jokes. Shirtless and disheveled, they barely glance up as my mother and I track through. My brother darts me a sympathetic smile, and I quickly scamper back outside. They weren't really very good-looking anyhow, and moreover they were rude. Creeps, I wouldn't want them even if they did like me. But the truth of the matter is that I feel gullible and naive, a fool to believe that any man would admire me.

The opposite sex completely bemuses me, anyway. The only nibble of passion I've ever had tasted downright sour. We were in fourth grade. Billy, Stan, and Kimmy came over after school one day. My mother hadn't come home from work yet. They knew what they were doing. We all sat together in my room on a little couch beside my bed. Too embarrassed to look at each other, we pulled my old green corduroy comforter up over our heads. Then for two hours we practiced "making out." I did what I thought one should—hugged and kissed, that is to say, keeping my mouth neatly shut and pursed. But the boys obviously liked Kimmy better than me. They kept switching places with each other to have turns with her. I tried to be more emphatic, more affectionate, more sincere, but nothing seemed to help. I felt like an idiot, and even began to wonder if, like the girl in the Listerine commercial, I had bad breath. But I suspect they simply preferred Kimmy to me.

She has always been the most popular girl in the class, after all. Ever since she starred over Susan Meringolo in the third grade Christmas pageant, she's been the darling of all the boys. Up and down Primrose Drive, where she lives, she's left a trail of broken hearts. She can afford to be choosy. She belongs to the Yacht Club. She wins medals at swim meets, tennis tournaments, and diving contests, and crews the winning boats in sailing races every summer. Her hair bleaches nearly white by August each year, and her skin darkens to a mahogany hue that makes her perfect teeth seem to light up her smile. Even though I rarely see her except during the school season, I've been calling her my best friend for years. Whether she'd agree with that assessment I've never had the courage to ask. I need her, purely and simply, to teach me how to succeed. So I think.

It isn't only the privilege of having idyllically happy parents, being the oldest of three children, and belonging to the Club, however. The girl does have charisma and, though I don't understand it, sex appeal. Since our adventure with Billy and Stan she's gone on to play games of spin-the-bottle in the Club locker rooms and to whirl across the moonlit lawns at dances until midnight. Her company is the older high school crowd. The boys ask her out on dates and to parties where she's learned to "french kiss," but more than this she refuses to tell me. She hordes her tales of romance in a way that offends me, but I make believe that I already understand what's going on. As Kimmy dives and dances her way into adolescence I perfect an aloof and falsely knowledgeable attitude that enhances my seeming precocity.

September 1965. I wait in the foyer of Eastern Junior High with a thousand others, most strangers to me, and pretend not to feel very nervous. The bell rings, the crowd surges, and my time in high school begins. No more boy-girl lines, single file to the cafeteria. No more tripping over kindergartners on the way to gym. The dark, drab hallways of North Mianus have given way at last to modern corridors, polished glass and stainless steel, antiseptic pastel classrooms, and row upon row of padlocked lockers—have given way, in short, to the promise of new beginnings, hopes, and anxieties.

But I expect too much too quickly. Popularity, praise, romance, gratification. Now it's my turn to rival Kimmy, I should think, but such is not the case. Junior high proves to be more of a social combat zone than a prime-time slot for me. Although Kimmy remains queen of one pack, she now has to share the kingdom with ten or fifteen sovereigns of other leagues. The greasers and the jocks, the members of the Gulf Point Club and the Yacht Club, the West Wooders and the North Siders. Territorial and class discrepancies spin such webs through the populace that it's almost impossible to get a firm grasp of the situation. I travel like a wayward puppy between the cliques and struggle to sustain an air of confidence and cheer. I imitate Kimmy's mannerisms, laugh at the jokes momentarily in vogue even though they don't strike me as particularly amusing, and dress in trendy John Meyer and Ladybug fashions (poorboy sweaters, A-line skirts, and turtle-necks). Trying to involve myself in the "in crowd," Kimmy's coterie, I avidly follow the cycle of couplings and uncouplings. Tina's going with Bob. Marty and Sue are breaking up. Peter likes Connie, but she's after Teddy. Donna and Patty are at odds over Tom, and he can't decide whom he prefers. It's a whirlwind period, I think, for everyone but me.

I'm either a glutton for humiliation or too hopeful for my own good, however, because I selectively make friends with the girls I most envy, the prettiest, wittiest, most sought-after belles in the school. Call it slipping in by the back door, or trying to. I hope that by winning the esteem and learning the secrets of my opponents I may beat them at their own game. I wangle myself into the network by doling out advice on love and lust, disentanglement and revenge, faithfulness and trust. I have no idea what I'm talking about, but somehow manage to sound authoritative on the subject of men. Perhaps if I hang around long enough with the popular people I'll eventually attract a suitor too. The boys do at least acknowledge me. They know my name and say hello, but not one selects me for his own. I nurture crushes on this one or that, plot with Kimmy or Connie or Sue to ensnare him, preen myself to please him, and drop hints everywhere, but nothing works. No one can explain it, but I appear doomed to social failure.

My brother tells me it will pass. He's come home for Thanksgiving. We sit together in the living room and he plays the latest Johnny Mathis tunes for me. Trusting confidantes, we discuss my plight, and he promises that guys later on in high school and college will beat down doors to get to me. He'll have to screen them for me and chase away the less-than-perfect. I laugh at that but silently hold him to his promise.

"You're just too mature for them, that's all. Too good-looking and too smart. Young guys are more insecure than you realize. They're afraid of girls, especially of those who act as sophisticated as you do and who better them in school. But don't worry, they change later on. Why are you so impatient, anyhow? I never even thought of dating until I was sixteen."

"I know, but practically everybody else in my class has gone steady at least once. I feel like an outcast. What makes me so different?"

I don't know whether to believe Scott's prophecies, but I do trust that he'll watch out for me, and that, for the moment, is a comfort. Despite the eight years between us, we're closer than most brothers and sisters I know. I depend on him to cheer me through parental dinner battles, to tickle me when I'm depressed. I expect him to brief me on the intimate details of sex that I won't discuss with my mother. He and his girl friend Sunny treat me to tales of clandestine house parties and drinking sprees. I watch them drive off in his convertible MG and imagine them walking hand in hand along the beach. Their life together appears idyllic to me. I wish that I could find a boyfriend just like Scott.

It is true that I'm impatient. I also, in ways, detest myself. My body is developing faster than the other girls. I am curvaceous and tall and, though not obese, am still my grand-mother's chubby little miss. Just before Christmas I have my first period. I've been dreading this since fifth grade when the school nurse collected all the girls in the class, led us down to a darkened classroom away from the boys, showed us an animat-ed Disney film sponsored by Kotex, and explained the miracle of our becoming women. We all smirked, trying not to giggle or show our puzzlement, and I prayed for exemption from the torture of puberty. I winced at the thought of the responsibil-ity, the mess of menstruation, and the carnality of sex. I went along with the craze for trainer bras and garter belts, endured the tauntings of boys as my bosom began to take shape, and mooned for love and affection, but I could not conceive of physical passion. The mere consideration of intercourse made me shudder with the memory of that evening with Cliff and Dick, and the prospect of the curse irked me. It promised to be a nuisance at best, an annoying intrusion of my freedom. The clean blue packaging of the Kotex box my mother gave me "to be prepared" couldn't fool me. It was a foul business no matter how you looked at it, and I wanted no part of it. Now that the bleeding has begun, my opinion remains unchanged. The first of my friends to be thus afflicted, I feel damned. My mother's gentle reassurances do nothing to solace me. She tries to discuss the issue, leaves pertinent leaflets and books in my room, and offers to answer any questions, but I don't want to talk to her about it. She accepts the whole process. I can't. I don't care whether it's normal or not. I simply don't want the responsibility. It's like a conviction for a crime I never committed. I vow to prove my innocence somehow and release myself from this punishment. I can't stand to feel so powerless.

Christmas 1966. The neighbors gather at the annual open house. They leap in age from infants to me, to young adults my brother's age, to my parents and their colleagues, and finally to the grandparents of the infants. Most of the merry-makers adeptly ignore the generation gaps. They fill each other in on recent successes and acting engagements, their latest business conquests, professorial appointments, and grants for postgraduate research. They ogle babies between bites of Christmas cookies, and discuss arts and letters, fortune and fame.

I feel stranded among these go-getters, too young to deserve a say, too old to merit attention as do the babies. Bing Crosby croons to me, "Have yourself a merry little Christmas." My mother's laughter screams at me across the room. She often raises her voice at parties to pitches that embarrass me. I'm afraid I would do the same were I to enjoy myself as much as she does, but since I can't seem to throw myself into the life of this party, I remain on the fringes and turn my attention to the groaning board.

If I can't involve myself socially, I certainly can gastronomically. Think I'll pass on the steak tartare, but let's take a taste of caviar. Not bad, not bad, but a wee bit salty. For the moment I'll stick with ham and turkey, bread and cheese, and a healthy dollop of Barbara's exquisite Swedish meatballs. I can never pass them up. And Eloise's cucumber sour cream dip. Well, of course I'll try it, a spoonful or three with several crackers. After all, Christmas comes but once a year, yes?

Snow blankets the ground outside and the fire in the hearth crackles gaily as the evening drags on. Bert remarks on how pretty I look, dressed in peach-colored linen slacks and a lacy tunic, my hair tied with tinsel and gold. As he approaches me I flash back on a photograph my brother took of me this fall. My pose in it derives from fifties pinup calendars, my ass in the air, my face tilted beguilingly toward the camera, my long dark hair tossed over one shoulder. I look like a languorous mushroom, puffed up and ready to roll right off the couch. My wheat-colored jeans fit too tightly. A pullover sweater stretches across my blossoming bust like an invitation to the rites of spring. I'm laughing in the picture, but recalling it I want to cry and run and hide. I feel a bit sick to my stomach, Bert. Excuse me, please. I'll return in a while. Why do I so abuse myself?

The scale in the bathroom tantalizes me. I know I'll regret it if I succumb, that this is not the time to confront myself with the old monster, that it's Christmas, after all, and why don't I simply enjoy myself. But the temptation overwhelms me. Gingerbread, eggnog, fruitcake, and all, I step onto the scale and watch the needle prance upward of 130 pounds. I can't believe my eyes. I know I've indulged and overindulged, but God! This is far worse than I'd imagined. I weigh nearly as much as my mother! The time has come, the walrus says, to pull yourself together. This is the straw that breaks the camel's back. I run through my stock of epigrams, but none suffices to lift my spirits or calm me down. How can I have done this to myself? Do I really detest myself so? I'm ashamed. The tiles and porcelain of the bathroom glare brightly. The fluorescent light refuses any flattery. My face in the mirror appears

monstrous. The hell with holiday cheer. I return to the party
and teach myself to drink my coffee black.

"Well, yes, dear. I suppose you could stand to lose a few
pounds." So she admits it! If even my mother suggests that I'm
overweight, the situation must be as critical as I believe it. But
how to initiate a reducing plan? The mechanics of weight loss
mystify me.

For Christmas, at my request, my parents give me diet
books and my personal bathroom scale. I pore over the books
and start weighing in every morning. One expert advises that
the dieter keep a daily listing of everything she eats. I buy a
special notebook for this purpose and proceed to enter my
daily intake down to the mouthful. If I can't locate a food's
calorie count in one of my five calorie counters, I refuse to eat
it. My plan is to keep the daily total below one thousand. The
books warn me for health's sake to maintain a daily minimum
of twelve hundred, but I'm more easily influenced by the idea
that the less you eat the faster you lose. Conservative wisdom
irritates me.

Fad diets titillate me. The protein plan is all the rage right
now. I subscribe to it immediately on hearing about it.
Nothing but meat, fish, eggs for a week. Horribly dull, but it
promises instant results. The days drag by, lengthened drasti-
cally by the constant attention this regime demands of me. I
must not cheat or forget for an instant my pledge to succeed at
this, my first totally independent exhibit of power. I conjure
nightmarish visions of myself as a fat lady, stock them in the
back of my mind as ammunition against temptation. Unpleasant as the undertaking is, however, it has its rewards. By the
middle of January I've dropped fifteen pounds. The sense of
accomplishment exhilarates me, spurs me to continue on and

on. It provides me a sense of purpose and shapes my life with distractions from insecurity. Calisthenics, modern dance, calorie counting, and schoolwork keep me occupied. I walk the two miles home from school whenever possible and horde issues of fashion magazines that offer new diets and exercises. No matter how exhausted I may feel at the end of the day, I force myself through an hour of shape-ups before bed. It's a routine I've extracted from *Glamour* magazine, only I make myself perform each of the fifteen movements twice as many times as the editors suggest. I shall endure this, I promise myself, I shall become an expert at it. It's like having a personal mission.

My mother cannot understand my sudden absorption. She insists that I quit the protein regime and, balking, I concede. But she can't dissuade me from my ultimate goal. There are other diets, other ways to make myself thin, and I intend to try them all. The constant downward trend somehow comforts me, gives visible proof that I can exert control if I elect to. It is the greatest satisfaction in my life.

I am losing my brother. He listens to Johnny Mathis down in the living room now, just as he used to, singing along off key and pretending to concentrate on his reading. We're alone in the house, my parents having gone off with Sunny's to anchor some last-minute plans, and he, for the last time, is watching out for me.

At ten o'clock I put on my pale blue flannel pajamas and went down to kiss him good night. He came back to the bedroom with me. I felt uneasy and asked him to check the bedroom next door to make sure no one was there. He didn't laugh at me, but went to check things out and, returning, told me that he understood my terror. Sometimes even he feels threatened without reason. You can never assume you're safe, because sometimes the most irrational doubts and fears turn out to be justified. Most of the time, though, they don't, and then you can breathe a sigh of relief, and go ahead to sleep. He'd be in the living room if I needed him.

Tomorrow is my brother's wedding day. The engagement was a sudden decision, but not unexpected. In a way he and Sunny have been married for years, and this spring vacation just seemed a good time to finalize things. They love each other, no doubt about that, and I try to convince myself that nothing will change. But I know that I'm losing a brother tonight, and a huge, terrible sense of loneliness overwhelms me.

My door is closed and the lights are out, but the moon shines like a specter through the window. It fills my bedroom with a haunting, cruel light. The strains of Scott's music reach me from much farther away than the other end of the house.

But he promised. He promised to chaperone me, to counsel and watch out for me. I counted on him to sustain me through the blowups between Mom and Dad and to keep me smiling when things got rough in high school. I wanted to show him that I could be his friend as well as just a little sister, but now he's leaving and I'll never really have a chance.

The tears pour down my cheeks, not exactly desired, not exactly checked. I feel terribly sorry for myself. Why me, always? Why am I the one to be left behind? My friends all seem to feel loved and secure. They have big families and boyfriends and their parents never fight. I just can't deal with this! It isn't fair that I should have to fend alone! Why, Scott? Why? The worst of it is that nobody knows how hard it is for me. No, I'm so grown-up, so strong. Everything stands in my favor—I'm so pretty and so smart. Mine are the highest grades, the highest scores on achievement tests, the best English compositions in the class. Of course I'll go to the finest college and become the best at whatever I choose to do with my life. I'm the one who pleases all of the people all of the time. Well, why then, goddamnit, is everything so hard on me? Complainer! Complainer! Shut up and go to sleep. How dare you pity yourself! You have no right to unhappiness.

But the sobs won't quit. I can't snap myself out of the horror and sadness of feeling hopelessly lonely and inconsequential. What does anything I think or feel or do matter? Louder and louder. I choke on the tears and soak my bedsheets. There's a modicum of relief in so completely letting down my defenses, but not enough to comfort me.

"Oh, babe. Are you crying on account of me? Please don't do that. Please? It's going to be all right." Sinking into my sodden blankets, my brother sits beside me and wraps me in his arms. He gently smiles and kisses my forehead. We are as close as we will ever be.

"But I just realized, lying here, that you're never going to live here again. You'll never be around anymore." I blubber. "Tomorrow you and Sunny will be married, and we'll all drink a glass of champagne and eat your wedding cake and then you'll ride off into the sunset and I'll never see you again. Not the same way. You know what I mean. From now on there will always be more important things for you. It's never going to be the way it used to be. It's never going to be the way I thought it would be. Oh, Scott, I'm so sorry!" I can't stop shaking. I shiver not with cold but out of a stark, paralyzing understanding that there's nothing I can do.

He tightens his embrace, strokes my back, and rocks me slowly, soothingly. He tries to reassure us. "No, no, sweetheart. I'm just as afraid as you are. More, even. But nothing's going to change between you and me. You're always going to be my sister. I'll always be here if you need me. It doesn't matter if I'm in the next room or around the world, and I don't care if I have ten wives and fifty kids, you can count on me. Shh, shh. It's all right. Really. Please don't cry."

Slowly the tremors cease, and through the dark blur I manage a smile. He has his own problems, after all. He doesn't need me to complicate the issue. I wish we could turn back time and play it over a different way. I wish that instead of Sunny I could ride off tomorrow into the sunset with Scott, but that is, of course, an absurd notion. So I pretend to be reassured. He returns to the living room to wait for my parents. There's a heavy cloud hanging over the house tonight, and my hurt feelings are the least of anyone's worries. I must buck up, take control, and redefine these smashed dreams on my own.

I throw myself more vigorously into dieting. My weight has dropped to 105, and my latest scheme is the yogurt lunch. Each morning I mix up a different flavor. Plain yogurt has many fewer calories than the fruit brands, so I experiment using saccharine, extracts, and fresh or water-packed fruits to make my own dietetic variations. I convince myself that they taste delicious. At lunch my classmates laugh at me for my eccentric eating habits. It takes me nearly a half hour to eat a cup of yogurt while, during the same period, the others plow through platefuls of spaghetti and salad, chocolate cake and milk. I lick my spoon at each minuscule bite and, reaching the bottom of the container, insist that I feel full. It is worth it. It wins me notoriety. I'm becoming famous around school for my display of self-discipline. My audience stands in awe of me, and I love it. Here's my chance to surpass Kimmy, my way of earning social stature. In this one respect, I'm the best, but if I let it go, all is lost, and so I cling to my diet tenaciously.

There are other desirable side effects as well that help me

remain faithful. My periods have stopped! I don't suppose the reprieve will last forever, but for the moment it delights me. And the more weight I lose, the flatter I become. It's wonderful, like crawling back into the body of a child. I have more energy than ever, can walk for miles, skip rope for hours. Unfortunately, there are also a few negatives to the process. I'm nearly always cold. My hands and feet especially turn icy and blue. I bruise very easily, and cuts and sores take months to heal. But these aren't such terrible sacrifices to make. I never get sick. I feel fine.

With what can qualify only as masochistic zeal, I attend almost all the biweekly canteens, dances at school and various churches in the area. Deafened by the noise of the "Sound of Rum" and "The Darker Shade" and "The Sons of Pepe," I tour the strobe-lighted gyms in search of partners. No one ever asks me to dance, but I remain ever hopeful, ever disappointed. I amuse myself by taking part vicariously in the agonies and ecstasies of those more socially active than I. Karen has laryngitis, poor baby, and is afraid to kiss George for fear of contaminating him. Debbie is crying in the corner because her boyfriend, Karl, insulted her. Kimmy is fuming because Clark won't ask her to dance as many times as Bobby does. Poor Kimmy. Sue nearly broke into tears because Teddy was avoiding her, but at the last minute he apologized. They've gone out to the parking lot to make up. We won't be seeing them again tonight. Niki and Dan seem to be having fun. They're newly in love and drunk. Whatever it takes to get you high, more power to you, I suppose. Look at Chris, for instance. Stoned out of his mind. He's dancing with Eve. She's dressed in vermilion chiffon and has painted a silver star on her forehead. They strew flowers across the floor.

One night, during a Battle of the Bands, I received my first kiss. Not at all the electric thrill I'd so long hungered after, it instead repulsed me. Jim barely knew my name. He smelled of garlic and beer and refused to speak as, toward the end of the evening, he drew me into a slow dance. I was at first so pleased to be chosen that I didn't notice how he drooled and hovered and plunged his hands down my back. But as it became clear that Jim was interested neither in dancing nor in making my acquaintance, I began to feel insulted. A little respect, sir, if you please! But I hadn't the nerve to tell him off. Before I could pull away he'd grabbed me under the armpits and thrust his tongue into my mouth. All those lovely scenes of passion between Clark Gable and Carole Lombard, and I wind up with this! Masculine initiative is one thing, but this boy was overbearing. He never questioned my compliance. Impossible that I might dislike him! I was simply a doll for him to do with as he pleased, coarsely caressing, grunting, ugh, and groping. Where was the attraction in this? Tenderness, trust, affection? Sex appeal? None of the above. His tongue, that fleshy proboscis, sloppily entered and filled my mouth again and again, and I, unable to assert myself, rigidified and endured it. I wanted to cry but wouldn't give him the satisfaction of wielding that power over me as well. Oh, why, why? It wasn't supposed to be like this. There was supposed to be magic in the air, fairy dust afloat, and pinwheels spinning halos around our heads. He was to cherish me and send me into rapturous shudders. The touch of his hand was supposed to send me soaring, not diving into the dirt. I the princess, he the prince, brave, loving, and true—that was how I pictured my first taste of romance. Instead my initiation consisted of an attack by a tall, gawky stranger who treated me as his brainless slave.

The day after my fourteenth birthday I take the first step toward a way out of my Glenridge snare. For months my girl friends have been suggesting that I could become a model, and the thought has its appeal for me. Glamour, glory, independence, and fame—what an ideal solution to an adolescence that promises me little else but frustration. The notion doesn't delight my parents, but they appreciate my need for distraction from my puberty blues, and promise to help me check into the logistics of the business. My father knows a famous fashion model in New York, a former United Nations tour guide. He contacts her and arranges for my mother and me to visit her.

We arrived at Annabel's Central Park West penthouse late in the afternoon. September was favoring Manhattan with a wonderfully rosy glow today, a glow that I considered propitious. I could fairly taste the freedom and success that this connection would bring me.

One would never suspect that Annabel had recently borne a child. Tall, dark, and impeccably manicured, she moved like a ballerina. She told us that she had gained and lost over fifty pounds with the birth of her child. How could she have gotten back into shape so quickly? She explained that she had simply stopped eating and established a rigorous exercise routine. Fifty pounds! My own accomplishments seemed paltry by contrast. I vowed to regiment myself more strictly and to polish up my image as well. This woman, after all, did not simply rely on her looks to make her beautiful. She cultivated radiance. Her hair glistened, caressed her head. Her makeup had been applied so perfectly that, almost imperceptibly, it sculpted her face. As she brought us tea her black silk robe seemed to float through the room, and when she settled back into the sofa and began to speak about the fashion world, I felt as if I were being granted audience with a goddess.

She reminded me of Audrey Hepburn, who has been my idol ever since I first saw her movie *Breakfast at Tiffany's*. Annabel is slightly taller and more sophisticated than Holly Golightly, but they both have the same awe-inspiring appeal. If only I too could elicit that kind of response, the gasp of wonder like the one with which I greeted Miss Hepburn at the beginning of her film. Wearing a black evening dress and in her hair a diamond tiara that glistened in the sunrise, she drifted past the windows of Tiffany's and nibbled a sticky bun, and I became her fan forever. I want to be her double, gorgeous, proud, and professional.

"Although I work without one, I think your best bet is to contact an agent to get you started. You should have no trouble being accepted. You're very pretty, and your youth may work in your favor. Admittedly, you're younger than most of the girls, but it can't hurt to get an early start. If I were you, I'd try Wilhelmina first. I suspect she'll be interested in your look. If not, try Paul Wagner, but don't let yourself be discouraged if things take a while. It's a harsh business, and it demands a lot of hard work, but once things begin to roll you should find it very rewarding." She picked up her son from the bassinet at her side and kissed his forehead. We took the list of agents, photographers, and cosmetics she used, and hurried back to Grand Central to catch the six o'clock express home.

I could make it! I squirmed and babbled for hours, too excited to do my homework, too preoccupied to notice my mother's ominous silence. I doubled the length of my exercise session and spent an hour practicing the application of eye shadow and rouge. It will be spring before I have enough time free from school to make my move into the agencies, but in the meantime I will study every pose, every beauty trick *Seventeen* magazine has to offer. By the time I complete my preparations I'll make Twiggy look like a hag in comparison.

Already I am as thin as Twiggy. Kimmy's mother is so concerned about my weight that she's offered to send along an extra lunch to school each day for me. I graciously decline the offer. Christmas is coming, and I must adhere to my diet that much more, in case I succumb to the temptation of seasonal goodies. I will eat nothing but dinner for a month in advance. If I get my weight down to ninety-five, I won't worry if I occasionally splurge.

But I do worry. I notice every bite, every inch of flesh, every ounce I gain. One day in the shower I compute that the average person consumes about 51 million calories in a lifetime. I try to visualize the quantity of food it would take to provide that amount of energy, imagine the power if it were all stored and released at a single instant. But I don't trust my own body to burn off everything I eat. I must consume less than the national average. If the underprivileged can survive on under one thousand calories daily (half the American norm), so can I. To this end I practice an ever-changing repertoire of techniques. No snacks, no starches one week, liquids only the next. The mucusless diet prohibits all lacteal products, and the Mayo diet advises one grapefruit half with each meal. I think constantly about what I can or can't, will or won't eat. I love food, yet deny myself. I hate food for what it does to me, which is to say sustains me. I have to prove to myself and everyone watching that I, unlike the average human being, need nothing to subsist. I must prove, in effect, that I am truly superhuman.

One week into the new year a massive snowfall affords me the chance to play the little girl I wish I were. Schools all over town close down. We are housebound for days. I struggle against the cold to venture out and build a snowman, something I never once did as a small child. Truthfully, I have no interest in the snowman, but it seems important as a symbolic turning back of time. So I don parka, mittens, muffler, and galoshes, and work for four exhausting hours to create the quintessential Frosty, charcoal-eyed, carrot-nosed, and top-hatted. When I come inside I turn my attention to all the children's books that at age seven I considered too juvenile to read. *Miss Bianca, Stuart Little, Charlotte's Web, Mary Poppins*, and *Bambi*, such treasures nearly forsaken! Back-track, slow down, catch up with lost illusions. I want so badly the thrill of innocence I missed the first time round. "I grew up too damned fast," I feel like screaming back when my mother amusedly asks what I'm doing. But she won't sympathize. We're never too old for snowmen, dear. She doesn't understand. I was too old before, and now I'm not nearly old enough. I can't seem to locate my place in time.

"Darling, won't you try to gain a little weight? You're getting to be so *terribly* thin. You starve yourself all day long, eat next to nothing for dinner, and you're so hyperactive it's trying just to look at you. *Stop* jumping up and down when I'm talking to you!" My mother clamped her hands on my shoulders to halt my jumping jacks. It annoyed her that I did calisthenics in the kitchen when she was cooking supper. This wasn't our first discussion on the topic of my weight. My parents have been pleading with me to eat more since they first realized that I was under one hundred pounds. But to no avail, for I am adamant. My diet is the one sector of my life over which I and I alone wield total control. I *enjoy* counting calories and feeling skinny. No one can force me to become fat again!

"You say you eat so much between meals. If you'd just stop doing that you'd have an appetite for dinner. Frankly, I can't see that you ever eat anything substantial. You just pick, and ruin meals for everyone else. What's the point of it, anyway? For God's sake, take a look at yourself! You look like a scarecrow. A little meat and potatoes couldn't possibly do you any harm. I can't understand where this ridiculous phobia of yours came from." My mother turned in frustration to baste the leg of lamb she was roasting for dinner.

"I feel fine," I snarled. If only she'd leave the kitchen for a second, I could get my business out of the way and go do my homework. I continued to hop up and down in the doorway. The hell I don't eat too much. It's revolting the way I eat. I'm never hungry, but I have this constant urge to gorge. All too frequently, left alone for any length of time, I'll give in to it and down a whole pan of fudge or an entire box of ginger-snaps. Or I'll pick all the raisins out of a box of raisin bran. And then I loathe myself. But how can I explain it to Mom? I'm too ashamed. She's too antagonistic to believe me. So to prevent the excess fat from accumulating, I do these exercises constantly and before supper each night I sabotage her cooking.

She gave me a weary look and collected her coat and purse. "Keep an eye on the carrots, would you? They should be done in a couple of minutes. I'm going to pick up your father at the station." She slammed the door behind her in frustration.

As soon as I was sure the car had left the driveway, I set to work. Taking the pan of carrots from the burner I carefully rinsed them under the tap, two or three times, then reseasoned them without butter and replaced them to steam. It nauseates

me the way my mother adds grease to good food. The cream
sauce she'd made for the broccoli was another tragedy. The
best I could do was to water it down. That would be too
suspicious if altered any further. But the lamb was a real test
of my artistry. I removed the pan to the countertop and slit the
skin open lengthwise from underneath. Between the tough
outer layer and the meat itself a good inch or two of fat oozed.
I took a knife and sliced off as much as I could, scraping the
meat dry where possible. Then I placed the discards in a
brown paper bag and hid them in the bottom of the trash bin.
The resulting leg of lamb, when I pulled the skin back tight,
was considerably smaller than the one we'd started with, but I
beefed it up by adding a lot of diced frozen potatoes, which I
could refuse at the table, and spooning juice over the whole to
give it a pretty, succulent look. I felt half guilty, half mischievous doing this, but I did believe it necessary. It would not sit
well with my mother if I got up in the middle of the meal and
rinsed off my portion of vegetables or if I scraped every speck
of gravy from my meat, so I had secretly to cleanse the meal
before it was served. By the time my parents got home, I had
vanished to the back of the house and immersed myself in my
schoolwork. They never noticed anything amiss, or if they did
they didn't let me know.

The next afternoon my brother asks me to help him clean
out a garage that he's renting from some neighbors of ours.
He'll be using it for work space. He and Sunny and their baby
have rented a small apartment on the other side of Glenridge
and, though it's comfortable, there's no room there for him to
work on his car, fix his motorcycle, or store his tools. My
brother, like my father, has a streak of the gadgeteer in him.
He devotes endless hours to automechanics and construction
projects. For his sanity he needs this space, and I feel honored

that he's invited me along. Unfortunately, the garage is too cold for me so my brother tells me to go inside the Campbells' house to warm up. They aren't home, but the door's open and they won't mind.

But they certainly would not approve if they knew how I behave. I don't know what comes over me, what kind of craving for guilt, this abominable temptation to sin. My brother works away, unsuspecting, while I, the felon, ransack my neighbors' larder and make myself sick on stolen food.

I stand on the counter to search for cookies, rummage through the icebox, use my fingers to spoon rum ripple ice cream out of the carton. What if I were caught? I can't imagine what evil motivates me. It's like a cruel seizure urging me not to release my Pandora's demons, but to ingest them. Pop-Tarts, Lorna Doones, Fritos, tunafish salad, Cracker Barrel cheese, leftover pizza, and chowchow pickles. I take hot dogs from their stay-fresh packages and eat them raw, pour Hershey's syrup into my palm and lick it off. I wouldn't put it past me to scrounge in the garbage can if it looked as though there were anything edible there. But the craziest of all is the way I attempt to cover my tracks. I nearly finish off the three-layer cake that was sitting on the window ledge, but I pick from underneath and between the layers so you can't tell. I remove all the shrimp from the dish of Japanese sushi in the refrigerator and all the turkey from the tetrazzini, then smooth over the remains to appear untouched. It's criminal behavior, no doubt about it, but I simply can't control myself.

And it's never because I'm hungry, but because I'm obsessed and, beyond that—I must admit it—because I hate myself. The other night, after dinner mind you, I baby-sat for the Jacksons and ate three jelly doughnuts, thirty-three butterscotch cookies, four three-inch squares of applesauce cake, five frozen sweet rolls, six slices of raisin bread, eight hunks of Muenster cheese, and a quarter of a roll of Pillsbury slice 'n bake cookie dough. It took me an hour to plow through all that, then I spent the next three throwing up in the bathroom. When I got home I swallowed five tablets of Ex-Lax and spent most of the night and the next morning in the bathroom. It is insane, appalling, reprehensible, I know, but I cannot stop myself!

Diary entry:
April 5, 1968

Biology, second period. I couldn't take it any longer, and burst into tears. Blank faces, insipid jokes, dumb experiments, and meaningless chatter. All these self-absorbed babies made me nauseous. They're like animals born in a zoo. Insulated and pacified all their lives, they have no interest whatsoever in the true condition of the world. But am I any better, really. We're all infinitesimal specks, individually meaningless. But each of us basks in his self-indulgence, pretends such monumental importance that it's sickeningly absurd. We sit in this cushy little corner of the universe, fed, clothed, and financed by parents who hardly ever see us and never understand us. We don't stand up for what we believe, if in fact we believe in anything, and yes, goddamnit, I am as bad as or worse even than the others. I despise them. I want out. I should ignore their simpleminded complacency and tend to my own affairs. I see what's wrong with the way we're living and I ought to have the guts to make my own way, but instead I keep trying to fit in, to hide intolerance, to pretend that I belong here. Oh, God, why can't I be strong enough to stand alone?

Modeling does seem a rather peculiar project for someone who spouts such humanitarian ideals, but it offers my only accessible escape. My mother worries. She thinks I'm too young and vulnerable, but I plead and moan and at the beginning of spring recess we make an appointment to meet Wilhelmina at her agency's offices on Madison Avenue.

Sitting with my father and mother in the reception area, watching Naomi Sims breeze past on her way to pick up her paycheck, I feel exhilarated and embarrassed. My parents too old, I too young for this scene, we attract some very condescending glances from the beautiful people flowing through. Each one more ostentatiously garbed than the last, perfumed, preened, pert, and perfect, they look as though they're on cue. I wonder if I'll ever be able to pull off such an act. My father smokes and studies the newspaper. My mother pretends to read a magazine. I fantasize about the day when I will sashay confidently in to discuss my career with Willy, as I hear the models calling her.

The intercom at the receptionist's desk buzzes twice. The secretary wags her finger at me and motions me toward a silver door in the corner. My legs quiver briefly, but I collect my wits and affect confidence on the way across the room.

The door bursts open at my knock. Bruce Cooper, Wilhelmina's husband, is coming out. He scrutinizes me for several seconds, extends his hand to shake mine, and tosses over his shoulder a casual, "This one's pretty cute. A little young, a little skinny, but I'd say we ought to keep her around." A tall, dapper man with a toothy grin, Bruce sets me immediately at ease. Laughing, I turn my attention to the beautiful woman behind the desk.

She looks familiar, but I can't immediately identify her. She sits with perfect posture and the air of an aristocrat. She taps out a long cigarette as she waves me to a seat, and lights it with the impatience of a captain of industry. Her smile is warm, but efficiently brisk. She speaks with a throaty, cultured accent,

European, though I can't place its exact origin. As she system-
atically examines me, I feel sure that she misses nothing, that
she knows exactly what to look for. She hasn't the stony expression of the stereotypical business executive, but she clearly is
an expert in her field. Of course! Her face seems familiar because for the past hour I've been surrounded by it. Reproduc-
tions of her cover photographs, enlarged and framed, line the
walls of the reception area. *Vogue, Elle, Bazaar, Town and
Country*, Wilhelmina was their star model for years.

She flicks an ash into the crystal bowl on her desk and leafs
through my photographs. They were taken by a friend in
Glenridge, some in my house, some by the amphitheater and
the swimming pool next door, some in the woods. I wore outfits and performed poses in imitation of Colleen Corby and
Cheryl Tiegs, and I consider them as professional as any I've
seen in *Seventeen* magazine, but Wilhelmina wordlessly hands
them back.

"You're going to need to pluck your eyebrows and learn to
use heavier eye makeup. Not much—the look these days is
more natural, but you're such a baby that it will take more
than you're using to put you in league for junior modeling.
How old are you, truthfully?" I lie, tell her I'm fifteen already.
"That is younger than most of our girls, but I think it's okay.
You're poised and mature. I think the teen magazines will like
you. But it will take some hard work to get you started. What
is your school schedule like?" When I explain that I live in
Connecticut and attend the public school there, she looks mild-
ly annoyed. "Most youngsters in this business attend professional schools in the city. That way they can set up their class
schedules to fit in with appointments in the afternoon. Of
course it's not requisite, but it would give you much more time
to devote to your career if you changed to one of these schools.

I'm afraid there's not much we can do for you if you can work only during the summer. That's the slowest season. There's not even enough work then to keep the top girls busy. I don't mean to discourage you. I think there's a good chance you can do well, and I'm even willing to try it with you commuting, but it's not going to be easy for you."

I'm speechless. She thinks I can make it! The logistical problems are insignificant, as long as I know I have the potential. (I would love nothing better than to move into the city, escape Glenridge, and go to a professional school, but I know without asking Mom and Dad that it's out of the question. I'll simply have to work on vacation time and whenever possible after school.)

"Hey, Will." Bruce pokes his head back in the office. "The kid's parents are outside. What do you think? You want to meet them?" Bruce seems to know without asking that Wilhelmina has accepted me. I admire their partnership.

"I'll be out in a second to say hello. Get Dovima, would you, sweetheart? I'd like her to set up some tests for this young lady. She has a tight schedule, but we'll see what we can do with her."

Bruce claps me on the shoulder and ushers me back to my parents. I stutter introducing them, but nobody notices. My mother smiles to hide the trace of concern over my grades, my health, my safety, and my future. She was hoping that the agency would tell me I was too young. My father looks flattered that his daughter has been selected. He heartily shakes Bruce's hand and I feel as though he expects someone to hand him a cigar.

Dovima, Wilhelmina's assistant, comes to greet us too. She wears her dark hair short and curly and dresses in a flashy manner quite unlike Wilhelmina's tailored chic. She eyes us critically, then nods her approval. Another hurdle down.

Wilhelmina emerges at last from her office. I feel uncomfortable in the middle of all this attention and am glad to turn the spotlight over to her. "Dovima, could you set up appointments for her with Art, Len, Bruce, and Ken, and send her over to meet Lynn at Dell. She hasn't any good pictures, so try to get her to as many of the test photographers as you can. Okay?" She turns abruptly to my mother and father. "You have an extremely beautiful daughter." I wilt. "It's going to be a struggle to work around her schedule. This isn't an easy field for a child her age, but I think she can handle it. I'm glad to meet you, and I'm sorry to cut it short, but I have a luncheon meeting in five minutes. Please excuse me. If you have any questions, I am sure either Dovima or Bruce can answer them." She gives Bruce a swift kiss and vanishes into the elevator.

The phones in the next room never stop ringing. Dovima escorts me in to meet the bookers who answer the calls and set up rounds of appointments for all the agency models with photographers, editors, and advertising agents around Manhattan and the world. The booking room appears to be the agency's control center, the bookers the real directors of each model's success or failure. The eight women seated around the room benignly nod, but they don't seem very interested in me.

Dovima tells me to give her a call in the morning. She'll try to set up something for the rest of this vacation week, and we'll see how things go. I thank her and, following my parents, flee.

We lunch at Sea Fare of the Aegean. It's late, almost two-thirty, and I haven't eaten yet today, but I honestly am too preoccupied to eat. Not because of diet, not for any of my standard reasons, but because for once I have lost interest in food. This is a benefit I hadn't counted on. Nothing tempts me.

Warm bread, salad, filet of sole. I am so excited. Not that it's a big deal, but maybe modeling will help me to lose more weight!

The next few days spin by in a merry whirl of phone calls and interviews with photographers and editors. They love me. They think I'm wonderful. Fresh and young, adorable, cute, they call me. *Ingenue* wants to book me. *Hairdo* wants me to do some tests for the July issue. Bruce Lawrence says he'll do some shots in a couple of weeks. Michael Avedon tells me to come back in a month or so, when I get my composite done. Not yet used to the refrains of the trade, I hear every line as praise. The sun shines over my Manhattan, and I feel like I've got it made.

But the end of the week arrives too quickly for any true progress to be made, and now, when I call Dovima to see if she's made any after-school appointments for me, I find that there's "nothing up." My mother, still opposed to the project, tells me we'll see what summer brings. Nice trite line, I think mutinously. My father keeps out of the discussion. There's nothing for me to do but return to the tedium of school.

Chapter Three

Lean Dreams

"WELL, you're just going to have to postpone modeling for another year. So sorry about that. I know it's a terrible sacrifice, but I feel sure you'll survive it." My mother, having just emerged from a two-day tantrum for the benefit of this summer's trip abroad, was in no mood to consider my qualms. It had required a harsh mixture of tyranny and stridence to convince my father that he should take us with him on his tour through Europe. He was going on business and wouldn't be free to spend much time with us, he argued. We could perfectly well fend for ourselves when he was otherwise engaged—no problem, retaliated Mom. The UN wouldn't foot the bill for us, he posited. We haven't taken a vacation in five years, she countered, and besides, with the money she'd made out of her fabric business, she could pay part of the cost. What about Aimee's modeling plans, Dad queried. His resistance was wearing down. Better go now, before she gets into it, she flashed quickly, it's now or never. And so he finally consented, adjusted his itinerary to include my mother and me on the six-week spin across the Continent, and booked us seats on a transatlantic charter leaving the first of July. I had no recourse but to swallow my misgivings and launch into preparation for the journey. The delay in my career wouldn't kill me, I didn't suppose.

It wasn't only that this dashed my hopes of an early entrance into the glamour industry, however. I was also afraid that this jaunt would thwart my diet and exercise regime. How would I be able to do calisthenics in hotel rooms with my parents standing by? How could I survive without diet foods and the steady reassurance of my scale? I shuddered with apprehension, like a junkie afraid of missing his fix. I wouldn't know if I gained weight, wouldn't be able to control my eating. I'd probably return home a blimp! By no means did this promise to be a pleasure trip. The anticipated strains and challenges were multifold: to be shackled to my parents, endure their bickering, suffer their complaints of each other and me. I would have to tolerate their scrutiny and concern, and remain stolid as they urged me to eat, eat, eat. Three meals a day with them, dining out—the very thought made me cringe.

I decided to take preliminary measures to give myself a safety margin. During the last few days before we left, I pushed into high speed in an attempt to reach my minimum, then drop beyond it so that if I did gain during the vacation I could forgive myself a couple of pounds. I was so methodical. We had shots to get, passports to validate, luggage and clothes to buy, and the house to clean. I made lists of each day's duties, organized every minute to keep myself active and away from food. The more hectic the better. My mother, exhausted from the morning's rounds, would drop into bed for a nap each afternoon, but I kept on working. Washing, vacuuming, dusting, mopping, any excuse would do as long as I remained in motion. I calculated that the housework used up at least fifteen hundred calories and my late-night exercises spent another three hundred. Add to that my basal metabolic expenditure of twelve hundred, and I was consuming right around three thousand calories daily, or rather, I was burning three thousand. I was eating under eight hundred. Using June heat as an excuse to dine lightly, I made my meals of lettuce leaves and low-fat cottage cheese. Although I went to bed starving every night, I kept my goal in mind and persisted. It was worth the hardship. It worked. By the day we took off, I'd made it down to ninety-five.

"Must you race ahead all the time!" My mother was snorting with annoyance as she caught up to me outside our Geneva hotel. "You act as if you're embarrassed to be seen with me. I can't believe it's really so hard on you that you can't be polite. Am I honestly such a trial?" Her face wore that familiar expression of pain and condemnation that at home sent me cowering to my room. Here, at midday in foreign surroundings, I kept my mouth shut and looked apologetic.

It was true that I surged ahead, and I felt guilty when I realized how it hurt her feelings. But she walked so slowly that it was excruciating for me to keep her pace. I wanted to move, to strain my muscles, to pant with exertion, to make my body work for me! I had no choice but to leave her behind at times. She liked to browse and window shop, to stop and read plaques on the walls of historic buildings. If she thought she might be lost, she would halt and worry about the dilemma. I would keep on going until I found a landmark or quickly ask directions and again get under way. Sure, I was interested in seeing the sights, but I was also out for the exercise. If she wanted to step into a store to price antiques or try on a dress she'd seen displayed in the window, that was fine with me. I'd just circle the block two or three times, get to know the baker who made the most beautiful brioches I'd ever seen, the local confisserie, the French restaurant that promised the thinnest crêpes in all of Switzerland. While my mother chose to handle the merchandise, I preferred to keep moving, looking, listening, noticing, and appreciating the facades of this time away from home. I felt like a colt straining at the bit. For the sake of my parents' sanity and mine, I had to find a way to dispel my excess energy.

At fourteen I hadn't the courage to venture out on my own at night, even had my parents permitted me to, but nothing prevented me from using the morning hours. As my father's official day began at ten or eleven, he and my mother usually remained abed until nine. If I could rouse myself at six-thirty or seven, I could get in a two-hour march before breakfast. It was the ideal arrangement, one that gave me an exhilarating sense of independence as well as an excellent view of the mundane—nontourist, that is to say—sides of the cities of Western Europe. I discovered the underpinnings of daily life in Geneva, Rome, Paris, Venice, and Florence, while burning off five hundred or so calories above and beyond my norm! These stolen hours seemed to me like secret treasures. I never told my parents exactly how far I wandered, and only intimated how much I enjoyed myself without their company. It seemed ultimately romantic to strike out all alone and explore these foreign streets, to watch the dawn mist clear into sunshine while the city dressed itself. I walked quickly, pretending to have a specific destination, and as I passed by, people would nod and smile good morning as if I were a familiar local figure. I followed my nose for direction and sought out the most colorful and bustling areas. My favorite haunts were the marketplaces, where I could feast without eating, taste without swallowing, where I could devour all the sights, smells, sounds of food in a vicarious orgy that left me light and excited. There were old women with kerchiefed heads and gnarled hands who laid out immense mounds of tomatoes, apples, green peppers, and oranges, all so fresh and round that they looked as though they might burst with the joy of the morning. Muscular men in leather aprons slung fish still smelling of brine onto beds of crushed ice. Wizened grandfathers with white beards and leathery skin sat behind tables laid checkerboard-fashion with dried fruits and nuts. And then, as if the sheer thrill of the street weren't enough to send me reeling, the bakeries spewed their aroma of the day's first batch of bread. I floated on that smell, breathed in gasps to savor the taste and to try and assuage my craving. I wished I could go on all day, but the call of filial duty held me in check. I always returned promptly to meet my parents for coffee and hear the plans for the rest of the day. But it was all right. With five or six miles to my credit already, I could afford to sit still for a while, and maybe even nibble a piece of bread.

There was, at least, no binging on this trip. True, the temptation of European cuisine was relentless, but without access to a kitchen, without any opportunity to sequester myself with food, I found it surprisingly easy to make choices from menus and keep my conscience guilt-free. My parents, unfortunately, objected to my overly limited scope of selections.

"*Salade niçoise! Salade niçoise!*" my mother would squeal in disdainful imitation of me. "Don't you ever get sick of lettuce and fish? It's sheer blasphemy to come to Europe and refuse to eat!"

"I don't refuse to eat. I eat three meals a day, the same as you. I'm full. I'm healthy. What's the problem?" My voice became icy whenever we broached this topic.

"But you turn sideways and you practically disappear. There's absolutely no reason for you to carry on with this absurd dieting business. Darling, why do you insist on depriving yourself like this? I simply can't understand it." She shook her perfumed head and took a final drag on her cigarette, then, stamping it out on the ashtray on the table, looked expectantly at my father. He was deep in his Michelin guide of Europe. The next day we would begin our drive from Geneva through the Alps to Vienna. He looked up at the boom of our silence and made his token contribution to the conversation.

"You really do look like a malnutrition victim, you know, Aimee. Just like those pictures in the documentary films the UN made when the WW Two concentration camps were opened up. Nothing but skin and bones, the prisoners were, just like you. Do you honestly think that's attractive?" He made a deprecatory face and turned back to the Michelin guide.

They were ruining an otherwise glorious day. We sat on the terrace of an outdoor restaurant in a tiny village named Coppet, across the lake from Geneva. The water twinkled in the sunshine and in the distance the geyser blasted sky high. A large tour boat chugged along the shoreline. Its decks were loaded with tourists laughing and waving, their sunglasses snapping like tiny black mirrors. My parents had finished dessert and were sipping their coffee. I was still lingering over my strawberries. *Fraises du bois*. Miracle fruit, so succulent and red, perfectly miniature version of the normal variety, but handpicked in the wild. My parents ruined them with thick clotted cream and sugar. They ate them in heaping spoonfuls, as if in a rush to finish them. How crude, I thought. I took mine plain, in the raw as they say, and picked at them a berry at a time. I would savor them, take full appreciation of them. I would maintain my habits, goddamnit. I liked my habits. My parents could not convert me, could not dissuade me from my priorities. Their concern only strengthened my resolve to adhere to my own scheme of ways and means.

But the most trying hours of the journey proved to be those spent cooped up together in a rented Fiat. I sat rigid in the back seat, my muscles tensed, my feet flexed, my back arched. To compensate for aerobic inactivity I did isometrics constantly. Suck in your stomach, tighten calves, press knees together, stretch your neck. Posture perfect, sit up straight. Trying not to look over the edge as my father shot wildly along the twisty mountain drives, I concentrated on improving my sinews. Rather than intervening in the fracas up in the front seat, I played internal games of stamina and strength.

"I told you to take that left turn back there. It's right here on the map, if you'd just stop and take a look. Why you insist upon playing God in situations like this I'll never know!" My mother threw the road atlas down on the seat in disgust.

"You did not tell me to turn off! You said it looked like the right junction but you couldn't see a sign marking it as the way to Salzburg." My father swerved onto the shoulder and turned the car around. He had to get the particulars of the situation down. He couldn't stand to hear things described imprecisely. His corrections always rang with accusation that somehow absolved him of responsibility, but they frightened me because they bore as well a tone of absolute hostility. I felt that I, by remaining neutral in this duel between my parents, was as much despised as if I'd sided with my mother, yet I didn't much care either for the vehement manner in which she carried on. But instead of pleading for peace, I curled my toes and clenched my teeth and ripped my fingernails to shreds.

Outside of Salzburg, in a little village by the name of Mondsee, we stopped to spend the night. Through the municipal tourist office we located a family that rented rooms to visitors. Mondsee had no hotels or inns, but the family was proud to welcome us. The man and his wife had lived in America for five years in Columbus, Ohio, and had returned to Austria with enough souvenirs to decorate their entire house. The walls of the hallways were painted turquoise, the floors were covered with linoleum, and the furniture, imitation Colonial, was laminated and polished to a sheen. My parents were given a room with a picture window and access to a balcony outside. From the balcony you could scan the whole valley, could look clear to the distant mountains. After the strain of the day's drive it was a pleasure to gulp the cool, sweet air and turn my face to the sunlight. I leant against the carved wooden balustrade and fought to block out the echoes of my parents' bickering. After all, the problem was theirs, not mine. I was merely an observer. There was no reason for me to get worked up over the situation. I should be able to find the humor in it, after all. But as I reentered their room, I lifted my head too quickly going through the door and smashed into the low-lying lintel up above, and all my pent-up anxieties became magnified in pain. I reeled through to my own room without a word to my astonished parents and locked the door behind me. All over the walls of this cubbyhole clusters of industrious elves were pictured planting trees and building cottages. They giggled as they worked, and some of them pointed their fingers at me. In shock, at first, I watched them, followed their antics, and resented their glee. Then a wave of pure loathing and self-pity engulfed me, and I broke into hysterical sobbing. I felt as though my brain were a crystal bell that someone had just shattered.

"Sweetie, are you all right? Are you hurt? Maybe we should see if there's a doctor nearby?" My mother wanted in. She rattled the door and knocked again and again. "You hit with such a bang. Don't you think we should make sure you didn't do any damage?" I muffled my moans with a pillow and refused to answer her. Through the door I could hear her addressing my father. "She's so thin, it terrifies me. If anything happens to her, you know, she hasn't any resistance. I think she'll be all right, but it's not surprising that her nerves are a little worn at this point. This trip is enough to try the patience of a saint." My mother's voice was scathing. I could imagine my father's sheepish scowl. What a way to impose a truce! Then back to me again: "Why don't you just take a little nap, and later we'll go into town for some dinner. I'm sure you'll feel better with some rest and food in your stomach."

I told them I felt fine and asked them to leave me alone. I didn't want any dinner. The next morning we proceeded to Vienna. Everyone was unusually congenial for the ensuing week.

Over the course of our journey we crossed paths with a number of my parents' colleagues, all of whom treated me with the utmost cordiality. In Vienna there was an associate of my father's, Sammy Piper, a gnomish little man who wore tortoiseshell spectacles and gabardine suits and escorted us to the May Festival at the local wine gardens. I found the black bread and cheese enticing, but cared little for the conversation of my elders. I wished I could go off on my own. In Rome we dined and cocktail-partied with several couples, old friends my parents had met in India. While I watched the fountains play, crumbled breadcrusts, toyed with my fork, and bit my nails, my parents and their pals exchanged raucous tales in remembrance of their past together and anecdotes about the intervening years since last they'd met. When we arrived in Paris we were greeted by another associate of my father's, a Ralph Meyer. Mr. Meyer was a tweed-suited executive traveling alone, and while in Paris had decided to do as the stereotypical American tourist would do, which is to say to go to the Lido. He assured my parents that there would be nothing in the show to offend their fourteen-year-old daughter, and so I came along to view an array of naked lovelies that indeed did not offend but utterly bored me, shocked my parents, and apparently titillated Mr. Meyer. He was kind enough, at any rate, to foot the bill of two hundred dollars for this extravaganza. For the most part, then, the summer's cast of characters took little personal interest in me, and vice versa. Not until we reached Lavagna, a coastal town on the Italian Riviera where we spent a week with two more of my parents' India friends, the Linnis, did I meet someone of my approximate age with whom I found some common ground.

Carla, the twelve-year-old granddaughter of our hosts, was also visiting them while we were there. In certain ways she bore a definite similarity to me, or rather, to the me of two years past. For she was a painful reminder of my former chubby self. Not that she wasn't a pretty little girl. I recalled that my parents had told me she had been a child model when she was five or so. She had long black hair, snapping brown eyes, perfect teeth, and wore sparkly gold balls in her ears. But her face was now a smidgen too round, her legs and arms too plump, and her midriff swelled like a baby Buddha's.

Understandably, she'd been lonely for companionship while

staying with her grandparents. They lived in the hills over-looking the sea in a sprawling farmhouse which, though comfortable and beautiful, lay miles from its nearest neighbor. Ancient olive groves stepped in terraces around the house. Pigeons, doves, cats, and goats frequently visited the Linnis' patio and entertained Carla to a certain extent, and her grandmother drove her down to the ocean to swim each afternoon. Mornings she usually devoted to reading and draw-ing. But during our stay she gave most of her attention over to me, and attempted to display her amity by inviting me to share her greatest passion—eating.

Midmorning, she would pull me into the kitchen with promises of a treat. I tried to tell her I wasn't interested, but she refused to accept my protests and waved the plate of flat, round, sugared pastry under my nose. "It's so yummy! You must try some!" The prospect of consumption pleased her so that I felt no guilt in declining her offer; she had enough appetite for both of us. Nothing appalled me more than the sight of an overweight person stuffing his or her face, and so I looked on with a commingling of disgust and awe as Carla sliced a thick chunk of the sweet, slathered it with butter, and devoured it. Patting her stomach and rolling her eyes, she informed me that I was making a big mistake to refuse this delicacy, but I commended myself silently for showing such restraint.

When we went down to Lavagna to accompany her grand-mother as she did the day's shopping, we would go through a similar routine at Carla's favorite café. She'd yank me by the hand and point at an old-fashioned cooler over the counter. Through the glass I could see a milky liquid smoothly churn-ing, stirred by a metal propeller suspended from the top of the vat. A sign written with fat black lettering on cardboard hung from the casing and read "La Bomba." It sounded intimidating to me, though I didn't know its translation. "What is it?" I asked suspiciously. Carla was practically dancing with joy at the thought of it. "Oh, it's like heaven. You won't believe it! It is made from crushed almonds and sugar and cream. Will you have a glass? How could you not love it!" I thanked her, but no, and watched, mortified, as the proprietor turned the spigot to fill her glass. Frothy and thick the mixture flowed. As she sipped an expression of ecstasy crept over Carla's face, and I reeled trying to calculate the calorie count in a single swallow.

One afternoon we climbed the hill behind the Linnis' home to see a shrine some wayfaring monks had built in the fourteenth century. It was no world-famous monument, but it gave us a destination for a steamy hot day when the grown-ups were all taking naps and we felt restless. As I watched Carla's round little bottom wag up the steep path ahead of me, I felt disagreeably smug. To think that once I too had allowed myself to slip into such a condition! Sure, I would like to splurge on the desserts and snacks that Carla loved so much, but I didn't trust myself or my appetite to let me taste just a little. No, no, I was afraid I'd keep on going and blow up like a balloon again. I watched the little girl ahead of me as she pumped her arms and heaved with the exertion of the ascent. It seemed to wear her out much more than me. Do her good to get some exercise, I thought, but in the back of my mind I had another reaction. I didn't want her to change, to slenderize, to look like me. We reached the top, and she headed straight for an ice cream machine that some thoughtful entrepreneur had placed in the small observation station there. I stood outside and looked at the deteriorating foundation of the tiny cubicle that was the shrine. What was it that caused me, though repulsed, in a way to applaud her unrestrained delight in food? Was it that the fatter she became, the more she stuffed herself, the thinner and more virtuous I considered myself? Or was I afraid that she really did have something in common with me?—that as my consumption might snowball into gorging, so her dieting might turn into starving herself, and that she might become thinner than I. That was it, I realized with a start, I considered this plump little twin of mine to be a potential competitor!

I needed some sort of concrete reassurance. I missed the daily ritual of mounting my scale, of knowing for certain whether I'd gained or lost. All during the flight home from Europe I looked forward to our first reunion. Like a Catholic going to confession, I was both eager and dreading. For twelve hours I refused food and drink, that I might weigh my minimum. Curled in a fetal position to quell the hunger pangs and trying to sleep, I worried over the consequences of the summer's dining. I had maintained my diet pretty well, had walked a lot and forsaken snacks, but the occasional bread and desserts I had allowed myself returned to plague me, and the warnings of friends who had been to Europe rang in my ears. Everyone gains weight when they go, they said, how can you help it?

It was midafternoon when we arrived back in Glenridge. My bedroom, dusty from a vacation of neglect, waited forebodingly in the late August heat. I tossed my bags on the bed and slid the scale out from beneath my dresser. It wobbled slightly on the uneven floorboards. I adjusted the needle to zero and positioned the contraption so that it lay flat, at right angles to the wall and bureau, exactly where it had been on my last weigh-in. No doctor's scale this, my nemesis was persnickety and would sentence me differently, depending where it sat on the ground. Move it an inch to the right and it would laud me, an inch to the left and it would condemn me. Only by locating it within the same precise coordinates every time could I trust it to tell me the truth.

I slipped out of my sandals and unzipped my dress. I could hear my mother in the next room. She had already started her unpacking. I checked that my door was shut tight against intrusion. It had no lock, and I could never feel entirely sure of my privacy. But the coast seemed to be clear for the moment, so I pulled my dress off, removed my barrette, watch, and underwear (every ounce of weight counted), glanced uncertainly at my naked body in the mirror, and stepped upon the pedestal. I closed my eyes for an instant—like a small child making a birthday wish—and looked to see the verdict. I had to stifle a gasp of astonished delight. I'd actually dropped three pounds since June. Not much on a scale of one to a hundred, maybe, but it seemed a coup by my standards. I would enter high school weighing ninety-two.

I stand by the wall in the school cafeteria and nibble an apple, my lunch. Though it's only ten forty-five in the morning, the room already teems with eaters. They stand, sit, lean, and ramble about, discussing their holiday romances and escapades, and setting the social roster straight after the summer moratorium. Between bites of sandwiches and sips of sodas, the members of the cliques appraise each other's tans and wardrobes, hurry to synchronize themselves with this season's norm. Out in the corridor they feed quarters into vending machines and queue up for the hot food line. The scents of beef stew and sloppy joes and Crisco and spice cake blend together to create a pervasive if not very appetizing aroma of institutional cooking. Ice cream sandwiches dance from hand to mouth, their wrappers waving like banners in the throng. Milk cartons, little highlights of red and white, sparkle merrily, jangling reminders of some continuum stretching back to kindergarten that I have dared to break, for I have not tasted milk in two years. But that's an aside—get on to the people.

Kimmy, ever the center of attention, sits with her entourage of football players, cheerleaders, and the officials of the student government. She perches regally on the corner of the table, her long blond hair streaming down her back. It's bleached almost white from her summer at the Club. When she smiles shyly at a compliment from one of the boys it's as though she were shooting an electric current through the crowd. Her admirers dote on her, boys fawning, girls imitating, but it doesn't seem to go to her head. The older she gets, in fact, the more the attention seems to disturb her. She is no longer as effervescent as she was in junior high, not so quick to laugh and flirt. She has a steady beau, a football player named Johnny Ward, to whom she clings these days, but the attention of all the other boys seems to make her nervous. Though it's difficult for me to check my jealousy, I can see how the constant attention might become a trial past a certain point. There's a rumor spreading through the school that over the summer Kimmy's looks caused a boy to die. I doubt, of course, that it's true, but they say she was walking along the street one day and this boy, a total stranger riding by on his motorcycle, was so stricken by her beauty that he ran head on into a truck in the opposite lane. I wouldn't want such a story hanging over my head, certainly. It just goes to show that such flawlessness has its drawbacks, and the expression of timidity and reluctance she wears on her face indicates to me that she's beginning to doubt whether pulchritude is really such a blessing. She'll be elected sophomore princess and ride through Glenridge on the Homecoming float, and the entire town will gawk at her, but she won't enjoy herself. She hates such so-called glamour, and one day she'll find a way to detach herself from the title her prettiness has won her. She wants to be known for some more substantial, more admirable accomplishment. I can understand that. But it's hard to envision her as an individual without initially concentrating one's attention on her face. I'll be curious to see how she resolves this dilemma in the next few years. She's bound to go through changes.

Three tables away from her sits a girl who has already initiated drastic changes in her personality. Candy sat next to me in seventh-grade homeroom and drooled over photographs of the Beach Boys. Once she even wrote them a fan letter and received an autographed snapshot in return, along with an invitation to join their fan club. I don't know whether she joined or not, because we were never very close friends, but I do remember her as a chatty, giggly girl with striking green eyes and auburn hair that looked as if it were spun from gold. Now she looks and acts like a mouse. Midway through junior high she began spending most of her time in the art room. She ended her involvement in student government and after-school athletics, and turned her attention almost exclusively to independent drawing and sculpture projects. Formerly boisterous, she began to speak in a whisper, to walk through the halls with her eyes to the ground and her books hugged tightly in front of her like a shield. Not that she ever held as exalted a position as Kimmy's, but Candy had her following and, to all appearances, enjoyed mainstream activity. She was a model student, well dressed, well behaved, polite, and cheerful. But perhaps she got tired of her glad-games, perhaps she had been adopting stereotypes to mask some deeper but more tentative self. Whatever the psychological motivation, within the space of her thirteenth year, Candy turned into a hermit. She gave up Ladybug coordinates for a new uniform of baggy pants, floppy pullover sweaters, Hushpuppy shoes, and faded green turtlenecks. She was always rather frail looking, but she lost a great deal of weight with this transition, and her complexion turned so pasty that she's come to look more like a ghost than a teenage girl.

"Long time no see." What a stupid way to begin a conversation with someone you haven't spoken to in two years. I blunder on. There's something about Candy that intrigues me. "What have you been up to? God, you know I think the last time I talked to you was right after you got the picture from the Beach Boys. What a riot!"

I feel self-conscious and immature. She looks at me as though I've insulted her. Her face darkens at my reminder of a past she obviously would rather forget. I'm sorry. It was funny, wasn't it, or was it. For her. Her lip curls into a sneer and she glares at me with an expression of repugnance. I cannot tell whether her hatred is aimed at me or at her earlier self. She rubs her frail wrists and hands against each other, as if trying to keep herself from striking out. She straightens her back to perfect posture and haughtily lifts her chin.

"I can't believe I was ever so ignorant. Pure teenybopper. What an asinine game. We wasted so much time trying to prove how cool we were. What was the point? It was all fake. Jesus, I can't stand to think about it now. Please don't remind me." She looks down to the book of Renaissance etchings she was studying when I came over. It's surprising how much antagonism she can pack into a whisper. She's indicting me for complicity! Why should I feel guilty? I've done nothing wrong. I never led her to the water, never forced her to drink. I barely knew her! But she knows and I know that in some small way I am still allowing myself to play the glad-games, that I still belong to the enemy league. For despite all good intentions to break away, I can't help but envy the popular figures around school. I would if I could trade places with Kimmy, but I can't, and I haven't yet entirely accepted the fact. I need, like Candy, to make a clean break, to throw myself whole hog into independent pursuits. But what?

Candy has her art. She pores over the pages before her, affecting total absorption. She wants me to leave her alone, and I will, but I want her to know, somehow, how much I admire what she's done. Yes, strange as it seems, I admire her gauntness and her austere demeanor, the violet circles that underscore her eyes. I am impressed by the long, intensive hours she spends with her block prints and silk screens, often staying at school working until midnight. She has the look of a stray cat, it's true, but I find her uniquely beautiful that way. Not like the Tiffany Holly Golightly, but like the one who sits on the fire escape strumming her guitar or who runs drenched through the downpour. Audrey Hepburn was just as thin as Candy. I don't know whether I'm that thin. I don't feel that I can be. I'm not powerful enough to be, not driven enough, not filled with enough angst. I want to be her friend, to ask her for advice, but I know that I must first prove myself as worthy of her attention, prove that we are really traveling the same road. I need to figure out what it is that we have in common, but for the moment our destination mystifies me and I back away, leaving Candy to her obsessions and taking flight to mine.

It makes a difference when I move into the newly refurbished basement suite. Neither my parents nor I fully realized before the strain of our proximity. Upstairs the thin walls between their bedroom and mine allowed little or no privacy.

I could hear them smoking and coughing, turning the pages of their reading and discussing politics long after midnight. In the morning they would complain if I turned on my radio. The floorboards squeaked and moaned when I did my exercises, and if I tried to stay up late to write in my diary or do schoolwork or if I were paying for an eating binge they would notice my light and question my wakefulness. I had to keep my moods in check to please them, though from the start of high school I've been increasingly temperamental, feeling very high and very low for no apparent reason. I was playing the role of typical teenager for their benefit, and they bought it, but in the seclusion of my downstairs room I can honestly open up.

Not that it was an easy win. The room, plotted primarily as a means of improving the value of our house, has taken its toll in grief, violence, and anger. My parents have sworn to divorce each other more than once during the course of the apartment's construction. I've been tempted to run away rather than to endure another evening of hysteria over how best to wire the bathroom or install the heating system. My mother has broken most of a set of Bennington pottery in her tirades over my father's pinch-penny methods. At the outset he insisted that he could do all the carpentry himself, to save the cost of labor and assure that the job would be done correctly, but he was working with such painstaking slowness that my mother in desperation finally called a professional. The carpenter built a bathroom and three walk-in closets to my father's specifications while we were in Europe, and with seemingly perfect workmanship. But my father found fault with hinges and bolts, and kept muttering insults under his breath as he made his inspection. When the bill came he stormily launched a barrage of curses at my mother and set off for the thrift shop, where, to express his vindictiveness, he spent one hundred dollars for a pigskin portmanteau. He paid the bill eventually, but since has applied his frustration against a rock ledge in the backyard. Attacking it with a sledgehammer and pike, he sends hunks of stone crashing across the lawn while insisting that this will be the ideal location for him to build a carpentry shop, if he can just clear the way. It is an ongoing project that provides him a convenient escape from the more immediate duties in the basement. My mother fumes and rants at him, foreboding heart attacks and accusing him of psychological desertion. Why won't he participate in the affairs at hand, help paint the downstairs room, for instance, or put up the bookcase or hook up the bathroom plumbing? My father ignores her. I watch him through the kitchen window as he stubbornly keeps his hammer swinging, his barely graying hair tousled by the cold November wind, his skinny arms and legs straining with each blow. He refuses to listen to my mother's supplications and ignores my pleas for peace. He behaves like a spoiled little boy, my mother like a dictatorial matriarch. Their spats should amuse me, I realize, but I'm too close to the action to laugh. And so instead I cry. The nearer my new room comes to completion the more I need to retreat. I have come to view this underground nest as a refuge from war.

The arrangement has a host of pluses, however, besides its distance from my parents' quarters. I now have my own exit to the outside, my own shower, my own telephone, and a full-length mirror. The mirrors, this one and another large wall mirror over the sink in the bathroom, play an important part in my life now. For hours I hold court through them with myself.

I hurry to finish my exercise routine before giving in to the reflective magnet. It's tempting to quit halfway through and get down to business, but I won't indulge myself. My plan is rigid, and if I fail to perform a single one of my scheduled calisthenics, I'll feel guilty. In due time I am done and can settle down to my nightly bathroom session.

I stare hard at the naked body and face that stares hard back at me. What kind of a person is she? What sort of character lies behind that pout? Is there madness back of that smile, or do I detect the glimmer of genius? Sensitivity, talent, ambition, intelligence, or pathetic lunacy and greed? Oh, bullshit! Why must I insist on analyzing every twitch and quiver! This search for motives and meanings is a drain and a bore. But it captivates me. Too many conflicting interests refuse to let me rest. To escape, and yet to fit in. To starve, to gorge. To model, but to struggle for humanity. To defy my mother, and to imitate her. To please myself, to please my parents. To rebel, to conform. Guilt! Guilt! That relentless harangue. What right have I to complain!

I scowl darkly into my double's eyes. The overhead fan drones on, masking the sound of my parents getting ready for bed upstairs. The Hollywood lights flanking the mirror illuminate every crease, every wrinkle, every hollow and bulge. My complexion blooms rosily in the aura cast by the peach-colored walls but I nevertheless look haggard when stripped of make-up. Ageless, with the cheeks of a baby and the gaze of a spinster. The puffy circles beneath my eyes seem to enlarge as I watch, and the tip of my nose turns fiery red with my increasing concentration. Ugly, ugly girl, how dare you even imagine that you can model! Hair like straw, swollen face, expression like a drowned rat's!

I pick up a brush from the countertop and run it through my tangled hair a couple of times. The object weighs a good pound and a half. It was a Christmas gift from my mother. A marvel of Lucite in aquamarine, it's more of a sculpture than a household item. Like everything else in this house, if I think about it. Everything in keeping with my mother's impeccable taste, everything just a little bit special. There's a personal statement in every ashtray, pillow, lamp shade, and vase. Even her pots and pans are out of the ordinary, specially selected. The furniture, which she designed herself, was made to order in India. The shelves of the dining room display careful arrangements of trinkets in copper and brass, marble plates from Assam, lacquer bowls from China, handwoven baskets from Africa, every piece a collector's item. The closets brim with ageless porcelains, crystals, and silver, and all through the house Persian scatter rugs litter the floor. Every detail is picture perfect, styled to my mother's indisputable standards. She has the knack all right. She can arrange anything—clothes, flowers, food. . . .

I throw the brush down. The counter shudders under the impact. It's all so sickeningly pretty. Love it or loathe it, what am I supposed to do? How can I compete with that kind of performance? I resort to petty defenses, nitpicking as if I could undermine her artistry by finding the corners she misses when dusting, or the wrinkles she misses while ironing. I sneer at her when she neglects to zip her dress all the way or when she forgets people's names. It irritates me when she sings along with songs, because she never sings on key and rarely gets the lyrics right. I can feel my gorge rising when she errs, and yet I know how ludicrous is my anger. The pretense of perfection is more mine than hers. She simply is and does what comes naturally. I'm the one that's the mess.

I press my face against the glass. A cloud of steam encircles my nostrils like satanic smoke. I stop breathing and feel the pulse in my forehead pounding on and on as I push harder into my reflection. I hunch up my shoulders and lean heavily on my palms, straining until honeycombs explode inside my brain. And then I gasp, released at last, and start to laugh.

I pull my hair back, twist it up, and catch it with a comb on the top of my head. Pulling the door to an angle so that its mirror gives me a rear view, I present my body for inspection. There now, it's not so bad. Still a ways to go, of course, but you are pretty thin. I bend to touch my toes and look sideways at the reflection of my spine, the vertebrae making a scalloped silhouette of my back. I stand up and reach for the ceiling to examine my arms. The elbows look like knobs between broom handles. I flex, and the biceps pop up like tough little cables leading to my shoulders. About face, now, front and center. I run a finger along my collarbone. This is one of the places I enjoy the most, the place where my bones show the most clearly, like an architectural plan of my body through the skin. It's too bad my veins show so. They stand out like a violet trail map across my chest. No, it's the bones that I want to see. Clavicle, scapula, sternum, humerus, radius, ulna. I still remember most of the Latin names we had to memorize for ninth-grade biology. And I can trace them now, can wrap my fingers right around some of them, like my collarbone. Wriggling my shoulder, I can see the individual movable parts of the joint sliding around each other. Then suddenly, taken by a fit of tension, I lift my chin high and pull myself up on tiptoe, posture perfect, the way we've been taught in modern dance class. Pretend that you're a marionette with a string attached to the crown of your head, that you are dangling from that string, that string is your only link with the puppeteer, the only thing that keeps you from plunging to the ground. You feel the gravity pulling you down, but the puppeteer's line is strong enough to keep you up. It won't break. He won't let go. But you feel that tug of war going on within you, that invisible power forcing you into place, balancing you. I open my eyes wide, feeling that even my eyelids are being pulled upward. My arms hang plumb at my side. The tendons and muscles in my neck stand out in exertion. My shoulders square themselves. My back straightens. I can feel my calves bulging and my thighs tightening. Then slowly, slowly I float down. Plié, relevé, bend, and straighten. I lift my arms again and pirouette, glancing as I turn at the outline of my shoulder blades and the discs of my spine. Pull down hard on the hips, and up from the waist. Pretend you're strung on a medieval torture rack. Harder, harder, until you feel that you'll break in two. The ribs stand out like stays in a barrel. I stop sideways to the looking glass and suck in my stomach and cheeks. Breathe out, pull in, tighten up, and try to get your hands around your waist. Nearly there. Good girl! There's only about half an inch to go until your fingertips will touch. You've got to keep on dieting and working out! It's so nice to feel skinny, though it is difficult at times to maintain the premium discipline when you look at yourself and admit that you're thin.

So I tell myself how fat I still am. I must keep losing weight. It's important! My face glowers at me, wrathful and accusing, filled with loathing. I slap my cheeks, so that they flare scarlet. Baby fat, baby fat! Ugh!! Wretched curves. I bend over to pound my ass, lift my leg and shake my thigh, despising every ounce of flesh. I grab my breasts, pinching them until they hurt. If only I could eliminate them, cut them off if need be to become as flat-chested as a child again. It is better now than before I started dieting. To think that I needed a size B bra! Now I don't even need to wear one, but the womanly outline still remains, and I'm afraid that if I should gain again they'll blow up like zeppelins. I would probably start having periods again as well. I would probably look and function just like my mother.

That thought taunts me. Because I don't want to become an imitation. Because I don't want to be such a victim of fate. Because I want to make my own name, cut my own image, set my own trend. I want to surpass her, not follow her lead. Losing weight is the one task I can perform better than she. For years she has talked about reducing, struggled with diets and exercise, but has never had much success. When I began losing, of course, I wasn't out to compete with her, but I must confess, it's kind of exhilarating to manage something she's failed. Now she pretends to worry about me, tries to convince me that I'm destroying my looks, but I know she's just saying that because she's jealous. I don't care, I enjoy being thin. This is the one time I won't let her control me. Or anyone else. I know everybody at school is jealous too. They all talk about dieting, but none of them has the stamina to follow through. I tweak my nose and wink at myself in the mirror confidently. My weight has risen to ninety-five again this fall, but for sure before Christmas I can get it back down five pounds.

We are excused from American history fifth period to attend a kickoff assembly for the school Biafra drive. For over an hour in the darkened auditorium we watch slides and film clips of wailing babies with distended bellies and tortured eyes. In one documentary a Nigerian soldier shoots off the head of an unarmed boy. A European mercenary tosses a grenade into a village shanty as the family who lived there minutes before huddles in the corner of the picture frame. Little girls run screaming through the streets, their clothing charred and tattered, their faces streaked with soot. Three young women, just raped, lie naked and beaten in a ditch next to the bodies of their husbands.

Danny Romeo, a class tough guy seated to my right, laughs at the sight of their bare bodies. His ignorance sickens me. I want to vomit, to demean him, to wrest him from his suburban shell, but instead I sink into the horror displayed on the screen.

My interest has a morbid twist that I can't fully recognize. I am actually envious of the trials these people are enduring. They have witnessed death, suffered pain and starvation. They have been to the edge of survival. The weakest and the unlucky have of course fallen, but the strong and courageous have lived on, scarred but strangely revitalized by their struggles. The mark of agony, the spareness of their bodies, the desperation in their faces make them beautiful to me. No martyr or sadist, I would never wish such hardship on anyone, but I do think it's too bad that we here in Glenridge never once have to run for our money, much less our lives. I would love to test myself against the cutting edge. I wonder how far you have to go before you know for sure that you can make it. How do you force yourself to the limit?

Walking into algebra after the assembly lets out, I see someone who looks as though she's about reached her limit, or as close to it as she can get without being hospitalized. She's just been transferred into the class and sits at a desk in the back. I notice her as soon as I enter, and react in much the same way as I did to the Biafrans, with a commingling of envy and dread. Her face is distorted, her mouth too wide, her lips too thick, her eyes too far back in their sockets. The skin stretches tight over the bones of her face, making her look like an ancient. She stands to sharpen her pencil at the window and wobbles slightly on insubstantial legs. Her calves can't measure wider than two inches, and her knees look as though they'll clatter if they touch each other. Her dress, though styled to fit and flare, hangs like a gunnysack on her wasted frame. She wears her belt tightly cinched around a waist that may be, at most, eighteen inches in circumference. Everything about her appears hollow, including her voice. When she speaks, it's low and raspy and almost inaudible. She acts cheerful enough, appears neat and cordial, but you get the feeling that something is out of whack.

What is it that draws me to her? As with Candy, I feel that we share something, a philosophical standpoint perhaps, a struggle of the will. She is clearly unhealthy, but she has some fortitude that I envy. She is so very thin! She is so much thinner than I. She mesmerizes me, but I can't find the courage to approach her, to find out how she's done it. Maybe it wasn't intentional, maybe she's been sick. But I don't think so. She's too lively, acts too proud of herself. She behaves as though she wants to keep her secrets, and I'm afraid to intrude.

(I never do intrude, never do learn her secrets, because before I can work up the nerve to approach her she disappears. Word has it that she's gone into the hospital, that her parents have sent her away to be treated so that she'll gain weight. I can't imagine how horrible that would be, but when she returns at the end of the year I can see for myself. She has gained, but it's all disproportionate. Her face is swollen like a balloon, her arms are like sausages, but her legs remain emaciated and her chest still concave. She no longer looks cheerful, but seems constantly in pain. It makes me wince to see her. How much preferable to stay thin!)

In the middle of the night the smell of baking bread engulfs me. I move in a trance through flashing lights, lavender, saffron, scarlet, and gold. I move down a long banquet table, past plates heaped high with candies and dates, baskets overflowing with croissants, piles of sugared crullers, and steaming masses of plum pudding. Down the center of the groaning board lie the entrées. Whole pigs agog with candied apples. Rib roasts standing with white paper plumage. Glazed hams garnished with candied violets and cherry rosettes. A Chinese chef beams at me across the table and bows as he lays down an enormous sea bass steaming in brine and smothered in shavings of ginger root and scallions. Crystal chandeliers overhead twinkle brightly, illuminating my path. The room, a Gothic dining hall, has been heated in my honor and festooned with garlands of flowers. I am propelled by invisible fingers toward my place at the head of the table. Butlers, penguinlike in their black tails and white bibbed shirts, usher me along, pointing out the delicacies I may have missed. There are sculpted masterpieces in shrimp fried rice, poached salmon glistening under a coral-colored mayonnaise blanket, great cauldrons of bouillabaisse and oyster stew. The scent of bread strengthens and blends with the aroma of sweet and spice. Another chef, this one wearing muttonchop whiskers and a billowy white hat, sets down a long pan of Yorkshire pudding. And then the loaves fresh from the oven start to arrive. They are shaped like hearts and flowers, or twisted into wreaths, or stretched to baguettes long and crisp. Raisins and fruit dot some, sesame and poppy seeds others. Some shiny, some dull, some bleached, some dark-grained, some even marbled. They come on carving boards with sinister-looking knives that seem to want to dissuade me from using them. As if to say it's all too beautiful to eat. But I really can't wait to devour it all, to make myself rapturously ill, even, as did the Romans or Henry the Eighth, to vomit so that I may begin again. I arrive at my seat. A tiny

Indian boy with an impish grin welcomes me and pulls out my chair. I lower myself and glide effortlessly to the setting that has been laid for me. Three knives, forks, spoons wait at my service. Enchanted by the acorn pattern of the handle, I lift one of the forks. It has the weight of sterling but lies like a feather in my palm. The snowy damask napkin at my left is folded into the shape of a swan and, like the food, defies me to ruin its figure. Even the goblets waiting for wine and water look menacingly fragile. I'm afraid that, as I did once when a child of five with my parents at a restaurant in France, I may bite on the rim and wind up with a mouthful of shattered glass. Something about this whole arrangement makes me nervous, but I can't quite deduce what. Lifting my gaze, I meet a thousand eyes and mouths, nodding and grinning at me up and down the length of the table. Slanted Chinese eyes, soft, doelike Indian ones. Thick-lipped African mouths, tight-lipped British ones. Ruddy Norwegian complexions, olive-toned Italian skins. The chandelier dims, leaving candlelight to fill the hall, and the spectators take the signal to applaud. Are they clapping for me, or for the creators of this elaborate production? Are *they* the creators? I haven't a clue. Then, both sides at once, my shoulders are tapped. I look to my right to find my mother, to my left my father. He pulls his hand away and turns his attention to the food. My mother grips me harder. She's trying to tell me something through this touch, but the message eludes me. It could mean trust or compassion. It might be clinging intended to comfort, or it might be domination. Whatever, she keeps hanging on. I try tactfully to free myself, embarrassed under the scrutiny of the worldwide audience, but she won't let me go. I wriggle in my seat, yank at her fingers, plead with her to free me, but she refuses and, rather than risk a scene, rather than insult or hurt her, I succumb. One of the waiters rings a dinner bell. It sounds a gleeful jangle, and a gaunt old man wearing a dhoti appears bearing a gold-leafed lacquer bowl. He sets it before me and namastés—bows his head over hands raised as if in prayer— and shuffles back a step. Everyone is waiting now. I feel my mother's fingernails digging into my flesh. In the bowl there lies a fortune cookie. A curious appetizer it seems to me, even in a dream, but it must have some importance. The silence and darkness of the moment thunder through the gallery, the only light a beam shining directly on me. I take the cookie and break it in two. It's like cracking an egg. The slip of paper flutters out, no larger than a Band-aid, but the words imprinted on it explode as I read them, become in fact bigger than life. My fortune reads: YOU EAT—YOU DIE.

Chapter Four

Thin Fever

"Shake it up, baby! You looking plenty good today." The pug-nosed truck driver leaned out of his cab and lolled his tongue in my direction. "Won't you come spend a minute with me, sweet thing?" He jerked a thumb suggestively. "I bet you move real fine." Scarlet with indignation, embarrassment, and fear, I raced to the opposite side of Sixth Avenue and scurried around the corner.

Hurry up, toughen up. If only I could just ignore them. But after two months of modeling, of trudging daily around the streets of Manhattan, I still recoiled at the catcalls and leers. Clearly, these guys ogled every passing female, no matter what age, no matter how attractive or ugly, but I couldn't help taking their hoots as personal insults. Was I doing something to provoke them? Was I dressed to entice? Had I smiled out of turn? Did I look the least bit sexy? I did my best not to. Cute, fresh, young for modeling, yes, but not seductive.

I swung into my Abe Lincoln stride—long, low, cool, and mean. I could cover a short block in a minute, a crosstown block in less than three. I hid under layers of floppy material, hunched my shoulders, and practiced a repertoire of facial expressions to show hatred and contempt. Stony stares to ward off construction workers. Icy sneers to flip at hotshot junior executives out girl-watching on their coffee break. Disgusted grimaces for the tough little boys who initiated themselves as Mr. Cools by grabbing and squealing. It was a strain to switch the smiles back on when I entered studios or clients' offices, but that was the price I paid, for I refused to take cabs and buses. The exercise was too valuable to me. At twenty blocks a mile, three hundred calories per walked hour, I figured I was walking off nearly a thousand calories, almost ten miles every day on my rounds.

"Hey, honey. Where you get your pretty ass?" He stank of empanadas and beer, and swaggered unsteadily as I sped on by. Maybe, I mused, if I lost enough weight, men would start to ignore me. Sometimes I felt it would be worth it to bind my breasts and veil my face. But if I honestly felt that way, what was I doing modeling?

That was a good question. It was really a paradox that I'd landed myself in this business. I who had such great ambitions of humanitarianism to dive head first into a career based on narcissism and false values. I might as well be a prostitute. . . . In a way, I was a kind of one. A commodity bought and paid for. Not that I was forced into this, certainly. It was all my own idea. No, and I couldn't use pragmatism to excuse it, either—how much money I could earn toward college, how great the potential for travel and future business connections. No, face it, I was a sucker for the glamour potential. It seduced me every bit as much as it nauseated me. Went right along with all the other ironies in my life: the way I longed to be beautiful, but hated to be flattered; the way I wanted to succeed, but to suffer in order to do it; how I detested privilege, but hankered after wealth; how I wanted everyone to love me, yet wished I could be totally independent. I intended to save the world and ensure my soul, so I submerged myself into the most worthlessly egoistic of all professions. Talk about conflicting interests!

I stopped outside Brooks Coffee Shop at 33d Street to drool over the cheesecake in the window. Another irony, how I dwelt on food and refused to eat. Seemed some days I never quit thinking of food. Brooks had a daily display of seven-layer cakes, home-baked pies, and this strawberry cheesecake that made me gasp with desire. I tried to convince myself that the cheesecake would disappoint me if ever I went in and ordered it, but that was a futile struggle. A work of art at least six inches high and capped with berries the size of golf balls, it had to taste like ambrosia. I tore myself away and moved eastward.

On Madison Avenue I paused again, this time to scan the menu of Esther's kosher dairy restaurant. It intrigued me, this listing of fruit soup, homemade borscht, Russian egg salad, blueberry blintzes, and vegetable cutlets. There were free matzos and seltzer upon request, it stated at the bottom. The prune-filled pockets and cheese pillows sounded wonderful, but then so did the apple crumb tarts and cinnamon streusel cake. Oh, some day when I was really skinny, I promised myself, I could eat such things to my heart's content. For the time being I'd have to settle for a cup of black coffee at Chock Full o'Nuts, and maybe, if I were starving, I'd treat myself to a Skinny Freeze, the frozen dessert that tasted like whipped mud but had, according to the poster on the wall, only sixty-five calories per serving. Whenever I asked for a Skinny

Freeze the counter girls looked at me strangely. "You ain't dietin', are ya?" They always made it sound more like an accusation than a question, and when I replied, "Well, no. Not exactly," they'd shrug their shoulders, shake their heads, and waddle away to fetch my Freeze.

But today I had no time to stop for coffee. My last appointment for the day was in ten minutes. Not that it mattered whether models were prompt for go-sees. Most of the time you had to sit and cool your heels for an hour after your scheduled arrival before a photographer would even put in an appearance. But I made a habit of punctuality (regimentation and discipline in all things) and always did my best to arrive on time. It made me feel responsible to adhere to an agenda. And it gave me a reason to walk fast and hard, thus exerting more energy.

I took a glance in the glass of Altman's window. I looked a shambles. Perhaps it was not the best for business that I walked everywhere. What with the ninety-degree heat and the August humidity, my makeup ran and my clothes wilted. My hair straggled, my sandals got filthy and worn down at the heels, and I hunched forward with the weight of my portfolio. Maybe I was crazy. No other model in her right mind would trek from 42d to 89th Street and then down to Sheridan Square and back again, but I did it as a matter of course. Besides, if I didn't walk, what would I do with the extra time between appointments? You can swallow only so many cups of coffee before you start getting the shakes, unless you eat to allay the effects, and that, of course, I wouldn't do. Nor could I afford to do much shopping, and most of the museums in Manhattan were too far away from my appointments to serve as retreats. I wasn't particularly fond of hanging out in churches, and my only other alternative was to wait on park benches, which would certainly fetch me unwanted admirers.

I had nowhere else to go except the agency, where I still felt like a novice, out of place and immature. That wouldn't do at all. No, I could always use the powder room at Altman's or Macy's if I needed to clean up; it was better to keep walking than to deal with time on my hands.

The mannequins behind my reflection wore skimpy knit blouses and long, flared skirts cinched at the waist. They were flat, thin, and tall. I compared myself with them and felt round, heavy, and short. The scale at home told me I weighed ninety-seven; I obviously needed to lose at least another seven pounds. There was little I could do to augment my height, but if I were skinnier I might appear taller. Is illusion the key to life?

It was funny. Sometimes I felt so solid and slender, all muscle and bone. But then I would see another model, or look in a magazine or store window, and all of a sudden I felt like a tub of lard. Walking, I could feel my thighs shake and my breasts jiggle. I would clench my arms to tighten the muscles across my chest, harder and harder, until it hurt. I would suck in my cheeks, like a high fashion model's, and tighten my stomach muscles into knots. But when I relaxed my body fell apart again, and I hated myself as much as ever.

Love, hate, love, hate. Which would it be? Did I consider myself lovely or loathesome? I could never decide. In some pictures there was no doubt—I was very pretty, if not ravishing. And sometimes when I studied myself in the mirror I was truly pleased. But the rest of the time I seemed as gruesome as the witch who once chased me around a childhood nightmare. I could stand to improve myself, that much was evident. I must work harder, lose more weight, and perhaps one day I'd fit the bill.

That resolved, I straightened up, ran a comb through my hair, blotted my nose, and fixed my face with a smile. Then I crossed 35th street, turned the corner, and headed over to meet Tony Y.

He was talking on the phone when I entered. A large angora cat paraded across the room and began to lick my toes. Tony lounged back in his swivel chair, swung his feet up on the desk, and nodded for me to seat myself on the wicker couch across the room. A propeller fan lazily churned the hot air overhead.

"Yeah, right. I'll meet you at O'Neals' at seven, then. I don't know whether this will work out or not, but you're right, it is about time I got a rep. But we'll just have to see. Sure, babe, I know, you might be perfect. See you at seven. *Ciao*." He tossed the receiver down with a casual bang and waved his hand for my book. "After you've been around for a few years, there comes a time to get your shit together. She's right. I need a rep. Maybe this chick can do the trick." He half-smirked at the pun. "Well, I'm getting sick of schlepping my own work around town. If she wants to try to do it for me, more power to her!" He shrugged and opened my portfolio. "Who are you with?"

"Willy." Six, seven times a day I went through this, pretending to know the business, faking ease. "I'm trying to get together a composite before fall. Are you doing any testing these days?" Usually you had to pull teeth to get photographers to test, but as a beginner I had to keep trying. Later I'd be able to fill up my book with tear sheets from jobs, but in the meantime I had to get some shots together to prove that I was worth booking.

"Mmm. You have a nice look. How old are you?" He had thick, chocolate-colored hair and glistening eyes. He looked about twenty-five, and he knew he was attractive.

"I'll be sixteen next month," I told him with all the self-assurance I could muster.

"Why, you're just a baby! You ought to capitalize on that

more than you do." He held my transparencies over an illuminated viewer on his desk. "You put on such sophisticated airs here," he said, pointing to a series of slides in which I wore dangly earrings and a long dress. "You've got this terrific little-girl look that's damned sexy, but you're not using it. This is a pose for a middle-aged housewife, not for you. Do you see what I mean?" I didn't see what he meant. I rather liked those pictures. I was wearing false eyelashes in them, and was standing on the steps in front of a Greenwich Village brown-stone. I'd done the pictures with a young photographer named Randy, a real sweet guy, who had taken me to a little Italian restaurant after we finished shooting. We had shared a lunch of fruit and cheese, and I had very much enjoyed that day! I thought I looked plenty sexy in the pictures.

Tony laughed as he slammed my portfolio shut. "Don't look so sullen, babe. The pictures are okay for a start, but you need to focus. You're trying too much at once. You can't be Oriental, American, high fashion, and junior all in one kit-and-kaboodle. Take your time. Relax. Get your act together—I'm trying to do the same thing, see? Let yourself go, and do what comes natural, just one thing at a time. Got it?"

I frowned. There was truth in what he was telling me, but I didn't understand how he expected me to follow through.

"Look. Have you got a few hours? I'm finished for the day, and if you want we could do some tests now, and I'll show you what I mean." He opened a desk drawer, and pulled out a bottle of burgundy and two glasses.

"I'm done with my rounds. But I haven't any clothes with me," I said with a sudden twinge of mistrust.

He poured a glass of wine and held it out for me. I declined the offer. I wasn't yet old enough to drink legally, and anyway, I didn't care much for alcohol. He took a sip from the glass himself, then leaned back and opened the window wider. It was stifling in the tiny office.

"In the dressing room there are some garments left from a shooting I did last week. They'll probably be too big for you, but we can stick some clothespins in the back. And we'll do some head shots."

Head shots. I cringed at the thought. You had to strip to the waist and wrap a towel across your chest, and nine times out of ten, the towel wound up in your lap, and you were sitting there center stage stark naked from the waist up. They'd just keep telling you to relax, that it wouldn't show in the pictures, but I could never get used to it, and sometimes it did show. Just part of the bargain, just part of the game.

Tony watched me as he continued to sip his wine. He looked placid enough. I guessed it would be foolish to refuse a test session so easily arranged. I could catch the six-thirty train home if we worked fast. It was now four.

"I need to call and let my mother know. She was expecting me at six. She has to pick me up at the station," I informed him. The expression on my face must have looked very matter-of-fact, because he burst out laughing.

"Mommy," he sputtered. "Oh, my. Yeah, sure. The phone's right there. Where do you live, anyway?" His eyes glittered at the thought of my mother waiting for her baby to come home for dinner.

"Glenridge, Connecticut. Wealthy suburbia and all that. Ever heard of it?" I wasn't too proud to announce my hometown, in the first place, and I tried to say it with enough sophisticated nonchalance to distract him from humiliating me further.

"Yeah, I think so. Isn't that the seat of affluent America? Richest town in the country or something? Lucky you!" We laughed from opposing sides at the joke of my fortune. "Make your call, and I'll go into the studio and set up the lights. The dressing room is through here and to your right." He vanished through a curtained doorway. In a second I heard his voice, muffled from within, "I await Your Highness with baited breath."

Did he like me, or was he ridiculing me? Oh, well, what did it matter? If I could get a few pictures out of him, what did it really matter?

"Hi, Mom? I'm not going to be home until later. I've met a photographer who's willing to do some tests this afternoon. I should be able to make the six-thirty train, so why don't you pick me up at Glenridge at seven-thirty? What? Oh, honestly! No. There's nothing to worry about. Let me take care of myself, will you? It's no big deal. He's perfectly okay. Why do you always have to blow the least little thing into a major issue? Just forget it, all right? Let me make my own decisions. I'll see you later." I hung up on her. If she'd just give me the benefit of the doubt and trust that I could fend for myself, but no. She was constantly hovering on the sidelines, passing judgment, worrying. I wasn't going to crumble and fall, damnit. I wish she'd just lay off. What was it with her . . . or was it with me. . . . Maybe it was just that I paid too much attention . . . cared too much what she thought. I shouldn't let her get to me, shouldn't try to second-guess her. If only I weren't so damned conscientious! Oh, hell! The hell with it, I would go ahead and live my life, and let her live hers, and let there be an end to this sniveling. Easier said than done, my dear.

I found my way to the dressing room, and turned on the light. Across the studio Tony was humming "Norwegian Wood." There were no windows in the shooting area, and outside the dressing room it was pitch black. "I thought you had to be somewhere at seven," I called into the darkness.

"Oh, no problem," he sang back. "We'll be done by then."

Good. Then I've nothing to worry about, I thought. Oh, for God's sake, why act so silly? What was there to worry about? Just because Mom's so paranoid doesn't mean you have to be. Don't be absurd. The guy's perfectly harmless.

I sat down and reapplied my makeup. The dirt and grime sure did build up over the course of a day. How could I, at age fifteen, have circles under my eyes! Jeez. And the way my face was breaking out, I was really falling apart. Mirror, mirror on the wall, who's the ugliest of them all. Oh, come off it! You're perfectly all right. Love me, hate me, spin me around. Christ! Shut up and stop worrying.

The clothes hanging on the rack were all wispy and frilled, with puffed sleeves and smocked bodices. I selected one with an elasticized top. It fit without pinning. It was little-girlish, and I felt sure Tony would approve. I was correct.

"Ah, la!" he cried as I walked toward him. He was lying on a couch in the corner, glass of wine in hand. Not to be moralistic or anything, but it unnerved me that he was drinking. Something about mixing business with pleasure. And also, it alienated me, put me on a different plane from him. I wondered if this were his standard procedure.

"Well, well, my little darling. Baby doll. Will o' the wisp, when did you awake?"

Oh no, what had I let myself in for. It wasn't that he was being sarcastic, or was he? What did he honestly think of me? I supposed I looked all right, but what did he want from me? Yes, no, maybe so. He wouldn't give me a straight answer.

"Scoot out on the paper," he said, pointing to the backdrop paper he'd unrolled in front of the lights. There was a winged armchair in the center. I sat down gingerly and posed. Prim, pert, and pretty. Tony held his Nikon up to his eye and began to bark instructions.

"Loosen up, will you? I don't want you to play a scene out of *War and Peace,* I want you to look sexy and cute. Relax, baby! Let your ego down. Get rid of those inhibitions. Play it with all you've got. Curl up in the chair. There's room for two of you in there, so use the space. Get your knees up, pull up your skirt. Open your mouth, close your eyes a little, and purse your lips. Think of the Estée Lauder ads where the girl looks like her lover's just about to come for the kill. Jesus Christ! What's wrong with you? Sweet sixteen and never been kissed? Why are you so uptight?"

It was true, I was feeling very uptight. It was dark and hot in this place, and I didn't have the vaguest notion what this guy was aiming at. Sweet sixteen and I might as well have never been kissed. I felt about as sexy as a drowned rat and at this point as attractive as one. I wished I could cut out and run. Why on earth did I let myself in for this?

My director set his camera down, took off his shoes, and padded across the paper toward me. "Here, kiddo. It's not so bad. Let me show you what I mean. First of all, pull up your skirt a little. Drape it softly over and up on your thigh." He played with the folds of fabric, his fingertips brushing my skin. Then he adjusted my position in the chair, to make me look kittenish. "And here, pull this down," he said, slipping the sleeve of the dress slightly off my shoulder and tugging the smocking lower on my bosom. "Christ, you're a bony little bird, aren't you?" He ran his fingertip across my collarbone, and turned me at an angle to him. "Now just lean back and luxuriate, as they say in the Sardo ads." He grinned. "Like you want to seduce me. I bet you never seduced anybody in your life, hunh?" The idea of my innocence apparently pleased him.

I didn't have to play dumb. I honestly couldn't fill in the gaps, couldn't fathom what was going on.

He backed off and set his strobe to clicking. It was unusual for a photographer to begin a shooting without taking a Polaroid or two, but apparently Tony felt sure enough of his light that he'd decided to dispense with them. Who was I to question him?

"Right. Now. Look at me lusty and bold. No, no. Close your eyes a little. You look terrified. Your man's gonna make love to you, sweetheart, not rape you. Lift your leg a little higher, and play with the hem of your skirt. Nice. Now look straight at me. Drop your jaw a touch, and wet your lips. No, don't stick out your tongue at me, just lick. Like you just tasted something juicy and delicious . . . say . . . a big, fat fig, and you're real turned on, passionate, and you *want* me. You're desperate for me to come right over there and make love to you, come on, come on!" He sighed and dropped the camera again. "I think, baby, you need a little coaching. Take it easy. I'll help you."

I was exhausted and ashamed. What a dummy I was! I simply did not have the slightest idea what Tony was driving at. I thought I looked pretty sexy. Just like one of the Revlon ads in the drugstore. I'd narrowed my eyes, pursed my lips, pretended that Prince Charming was about to descend. What did this guy want from me? Sure, go ahead and show me. It was a cinch I couldn't get it on my own.

He got down on his knees in front of me, and tipped my chin back slightly. He looked extremely businesslike. I felt stupid. He cocked my head to the right, and parted my lips with his forefinger. He looked me dead in the eye as he brought his mouth closer and closer. I was tempted to burst out laughing, but he acted so serious about the whole thing that I didn't dare. His hands went down on my hips as he put his mouth to mine. It didn't feel like a kiss exactly. It was too slobbery and insistent. He thrust his tongue inside my mouth. It felt like he was ramming a gigantic cigar down my throat. I couldn't breathe.

"There, you see!" he cried, leaping back across the studio. I saw nothing. I was gasping for air, and feeling like I must be blue in the face. But he grabbed up his camera and began to snap pictures like a madman. "Breathless! Impassioned! Astonished! You're beautiful, babe, really great!" He finished the roll and told me to go take my dress off, wrap a towel around myself, and we'd do some head shots.

I was still stunned by his attack. Had he just put some weird sort of make on me, or had he really been using that as a way to elicit a pose? I felt shaken by his kiss. I hadn't enjoyed it at all, but on the other hand, I didn't have any real grounds to accuse him, either. Befuddled, I retreated to the dressing room to strip.

By the time I returned, however, he had devised a plan other than the normal head shot. He had spread sheaths of cellophane across the floor. A box of big, brightly colored crayons lay by his side. I couldn't imagine what he had in mind, and I was not at all sure I was going to approve of it. Still, I couldn't see how I could refuse to comply. I would just have to pretend, whatever it was, that it didn't faze me.

"Ordinary heads are so boring," he announced upon seeing me. I clung to my towel, my sarong. "I picked up these body paints last week, and I've been curious to see how they work. If we wrap you in this plastic and paint you up a bit, I think we may get a terrific effect. What do you think?" I kept my mouth shut. "Now, just sit on the floor here, and we'll have a little artistic session."

I took one long turn through my never-never land of panic

and numbed my mind to the proceedings. Let him play his games with my body. I would be elsewhere.

He first set to work on my face and head. He wet back my hair, and colored my eyelids lunar green and my lips alizarin crimson. Then he pulled back to admire his work, smacked his lips, and removed my towel. Starting below my left armpit, he wove the cellophane around my torso, between my legs, and tucked the ends in back. I felt nothing as he yanked the arrangement into place, but marveled from a distance at the fiendish exuberance, the impatient dexterity with which he worked. He babbled as though in an amphetamine fervor. And when he finished binding my body, he opened his magic box.

I could smell his sweat and noticed that his hands were shaking as he began to draw concentric circles, whorls, and patches of color wherever my skin was exposed. He kept saying how fabulous the effect would be, what sweet little breasts I had, and what an enticing ass. My crotch itched. He kept sticking crayons underneath the plastic to reach certain out-of-the-way spots. If I squirmed he dug harder into my flesh. He was intent on his work and did not once look at my face to see how I was faring throughout this experiment. From my viewpoint all I could see of the proceedings were the top of his head with its greasy hair, the back of his rumpled Ban-lon shirt, and two hands very stumpy and fat.

I sat up abruptly, almost knocking the crayon out of his fist, and told him that it was getting late. He was breathing heavily, almost panting, and he gnashed his teeth as he consented to begin shooting. I knew before we began that I'd just as soon never see the results.

He sent me back out on the set and ordered me to sit on the floor and arch my back, hands behind me for support, my face lifted to the ceiling. When he hit the strobes, the plastic flashed, blinding me. I made believe they were the northern lights dancing around my head, that I was alone deep in some primeval forest. I was bundled in sweaters and blankets for warmth, and my heart was racing with the challenge of my solitude. I watched the sky flickering rose and sapphire and gold, but felt the more immediate darkness shrouding me from harm.

"Make Hiro look like an amateur, I tell you. Honey, these shots are brilliant, if I do say so myself." Tony rushed out, coming at me like a hungry elk from my imaginary woodland. He grabbed me by the shoulders and planted an aggressive kiss on my mouth. I straightened up, snapping abruptly out of my reverie, and clutched for my towel.

I still had nothing specific to hold against him, but I felt violated, nevertheless. And stupid and cheap. Face it, it was my own fault. He'd said it himself—he wasn't going to rape me. But for my money he might as well have.

"What time is it," I demanded coldly.

"Hail, commandant!" he quipped, flinging me a mock salute. "It's not even five-thirty. You have plenty of time to run for your train and trundle home to Mummy and Daddy. You were splendid, sweet pea, so what's the scene all about? No problem, right?" He held up his hands as though in surrender. "Look, you're still in one piece. And a virgin, to boot!" His mouth twitched with the joke of it all. I ran for the dressing room, half expecting him to follow. But he didn't, and I quickly changed, packed up my belongings, grabbed my portfolio, and sped for the exit.

"I'll call you about the contact sheet sometime next week," I flung over my shoulder and fled. But though I did call, the contact sheet was never processed, and I never again saw or heard from Tony Y.

It was a cheaper shot than even he probably realized. To him I was simply a quick-change doll. One in a million, like an inflatable mannequin advertised in the back of a porno magazine. Designed to twist and turn to the tune of his pleasure. It wouldn't bother me if he played awhile. Certainly not. I'd just go on, a fun-loving little kid, go on home to the folks, go on to dabble part-time at modeling. I was a rich suburban brat who would probably wind up in some expensive junior college and then go find a husband to foot the bill for the rest of my life. What difference would it make if he, Tony, got a few kicks from me one afternoon before I figured out what was what. If I ever would. He was a big-shot photographer, after all, and a few knock-ups, of one sort or another, were part of the bargain for any aspiring young model.

Sure, just like the catcalls were the price you paid to walk down the street. God, how I hated men! They made my skin crawl. Worse. They made me despise myself, my body, my sex. They were bastards, it was true, but mine was the flesh that teased them. Ugh, what an abominable business. There had to be a way out. To become androgynous.

All the way home I plotted. To starve seemed the best way. To starve myself beyond recognition. Oh, hell. Could I do it? I was so damned weak. I gave in at the drop of a hat. It took resistance and fortitude. . . . I sat rigid and furious, glaring out at the smug suburban twilight racing to meet me. "We're all in our places with sunshiny faces"—that was the song my mother used to sing to me in the morning when I was little. Well, I was no place now, maybe never had been, and I definitely did not have a sunshiny face anymore. Oh, I could smile and beguile to beat the band. Yes, I could play Patty Playpal and Goody Two Shoes and Red Riding Hood walking straight to the jaws of the wolf. I could be charming or dumb or delicious on command, but inside I could feel razor blades slashing. Wind-up doll, that was the role I kept playing. And I did it to myself. I tried to read people's minds, to find out what they wanted me to do. They didn't even have to push—I'd beat them to the punch! No, nobody forced me to make straight A's, or keep my room clean, or keep a regimented list in my diary of every person, place, and thing that cluttered my life. Mom didn't demand that I earn my own money. Dad didn't insist that I go on to college. Most of my teachers didn't even seem to care whether or not I turned up for classes—I could do the work on my own time just as well, they said. No, the compulsions were my own problem, my very own doing. Tony had made no effort to force me. I could have walked out, could have turned the tide to suit me at any point, but no. I didn't have the guts to take a stand. I just let him walk all over me. No control! No control! Red lights flashing and sirens screaming. Even the goons on the street had me the way they wanted me. I could just see them laughing themselves sick as they watched me, the scared little rabbit, scurrying away. Give 'em hell, why don't you! No, to take them by surprise was not my way, not my way to rebel or to talk back. Don't protest the appointed character, 'cause somebody might not approve. Well, all right, if I can't strike out, I can strike inside. Quiet and stealthy, shock treatment. Discipline. So skinny that men won't want me, that everybody will quit assuming that everything comes so damned easy for me, that I'm so perfect! Nothing comes easy for *me*. It comes easy for the good girl they've designed with their ideal images. Oh, I was great at parody, but this time I'd show them that there was more to me than imitation this and that. Ha! Show them that less is more!

I'd been tearing at my fingernails, and the cuticles were bleeding. I pressed them with Kleenex until they stopped, then lifted a sheaf of hair from my shoulder. The split ends sparkled in the fading light as we pulled to a stop at the Rye station. Ten minutes and I'd be home to turn on the carefree-nothing's-wrong face I always wore to greet Mom and Dad. They would never learn about Tony Y. I selected a single hair to play with. It looked at close range like a splayed feather. It looked like death, all dried out and broken. I took a single filament between my fingertips and pulled it from the main shaft. Gently, gently, like blowing a bubble, to make it last as long as I could. The object of the game was to halve the whole, to get the pull to last to the scalp. Which side would be the shorter? Like when you pulled at a turkey bone, you never could be sure whose side would break off. Sometimes the strength of the hair switched halfway up, and the filament you'd supposed the weakest turned out to be the mainline. Odd what pleasure I got from ripping it apart. But the thread broke at last, and the obviously weaker end did break off. It curled in my palm, a microscopic spring. I yanked the rest of the hair out too. It was almost a foot long, and looked as though it had been through the wars. I laid it to rest across my lap and smirked at my depravity. Games, games, such sick, childish games.

"Glenridge! Glenn Reedge!" called the conductor. "Last call for Glenridge!" I gathered up my portfolio and carryall, and waited with a smile for the door to open.

No matter what, you must keep smiling. Through jealousy, fear, frustration, disgust, you must never show the traces of emotion. Play cute and sweet and young. Don't let Them know that you think or worry, because that would make Them question your motives, and you'd be stymied as to what to answer. Why, Miss Liu, do you wish to model? How can I explain that it's part of an escape plot? From Glenridge, from my parents, from myself. Can't, so best keep those dimples dimpling, and let Them think that I'm just like all the other sparkly teenyboppers, fresh in from the Miss Omaha Model's Contest, come to the Big Apple for the glamour and the whirl.

It's not really like that. It's exhausting and cruel. The girls who strike it rich are skinny, vivacious, catty, and confident. So they seem to me, anyway, whenever we work together.

I am sometimes booked with the pros. Like sleek felines, they sit before dressing-room mirrors and apply their makeup. They chatter about boyfriends, location shootings in the Bahamas, vacations in Paris, and where's the best place to buy an oversized calfskin satchel. They make a point of excluding me from their clique. The client—Montgomery Ward, Bobbie Brooks, *Seventeen,* or Sears—may have hired me, but that doesn't mean that these girls have to acknowledge me. They can tell I won't last long.

I improvise gestures with mascara and lipstick wands, and wonder what makes them such winners. How should I try to compete?

We go out on the set when they're ready, and position ourselves as Sante, the photographer, directs us. A stylist hurries in to pin the garments so they'll hang properly, which is to say like cardboard. Colleen and Lucy giggle at a private joke, then strike a practiced pose. I wait for somebody to tell me what to do. The art director squints at me, as if to inform me that I'm the stray cat and what-am-I-going-to-do-about-it. Sante snaps at me to kneel and look up at Shelley. His assistant hooks up the strobe and shoots a couple of Polaroids. While another assistant fiddles with the lights, the stylist adjusts a bow in my hair. My legs ache. My kneecaps grate against the concrete floor, and my stomach grumbles with hunger. It's after noon, and I haven't eaten in twenty hours. I skipped dinner last night so my stomach would be flat for this shooting, but I feel now like I may pass out. Shelley beats me to it.

As she faints she falls off the stool next to me and brushes against my hand. I can feel the delicacy of her body at a touch. Is that fragility the key to her success? Sante halts the shooting and sends to a local coffee shop for food.

Shelley's lunch consists of an egg salad sandwich, yogurt, an apple, and milk. Colleen and Lucy have each ordered hamburgers, potato chips, and Cokes, which they wolf down in minutes. I watch, mesmerized and horrified. It seems to me enough food for an army, but these girls are like toothpicks, flat and narrow. How can they possibly eat so much and look like that? I bet they never binge, but still it seems unfair. I play with my vinegared lettuce and sip my black coffee and listen to their insignificant chatter.

After eating, Shelley assures everyone that she feels fine, and we begin to shoot again. My eyes smart from the glare of the lights, and my throat burns from the acid of my lunch, but I give a toothy grin. To keep my face animated I carry on a nonsensical conversation with myself. I think I must look like an ass, but Sante makes no comment on my performance one way or the other. He calls me You. He addresses the others by name. I get the message and quietly do my job. Must they rub it in? (Now, now, dear. You're taking this all much too personally. Surely you don't think they're taking special pains to make you feel bad? They couldn't care less. They don't even see you. You're just here to fill the space and to make the stars shine that much brighter. You should be grateful you're getting any work at all. Oh, you're cute and all. Still got your baby fat, though, and you're too short and Eurasian as well. Not like Shelley. She's got it made, just look at her. Sleek, fair, agile, and tall. Blond and blue-eyed, she looks like a golden reed. Makes you look like a fat slob, kiddo.)

But despite the unspoken—and probably unintentional—slights, I keep on modeling. When school begins I accept appointments after class hours and skip classes whenever bookings come up. When my picture appears in magazines I bask in the praise of impressed classmates. They, so ignorant, consider me a celebrity. I report the thrill of their admiration to my diary:

> My picture is in this month's *Ingenue*, and on the cover of *American Girl*. Everybody at school made such a fuss. I honestly felt like I had some status. At least they recognize me, and that gives me some degree of confidence. Usually I'm lost in that twittering maze of adorable girls, all so much more fashionable for love than I, but for once I have the spotlight, and the whole school is paying attention.

Especially among the girls, I begin to realize, I have admirers.

One afternoon early in the spring of our junior year, Kimmy walked home with me after school. It had been a long while since we last talked, and at first we struggled over shared memories of childhood birthday parties and primary school. I felt privileged to have her company to myself. She usually had such a thick group around her that an outsider to the clique, as I was, couldn't get through. But today, for some reason, she had singled me out as I left the school grounds, had followed me and asked if she could join me on the way home. I asked if she was sure she wanted to walk the whole way. It was far, over five miles, and though I walked it every day in my seemingly hopeless attempt to lose ever more weight, I never expected anybody else to want such exercise. In fact, I secretly guarded the privilege for myself as proof of my independence, superior stamina, and will. But for Kimmy I would open up and share the two-hour jaunt.

The leaves above us glimmered in the sunshine. The leap into spring always filled me with energy and determination to carry through on my promise to make myself skinny. It was such an important goal for me. Why, then, so difficult to realize? Well, with another summer of modeling coming up, I would steel myself. All through the winter I'd been able to keep my weight at ninety-seven through successive binges—oh, why, did I despise myself so?—but despite the laxatives, exercise, and vomiting that followed them, I couldn't drop back to the ninety-two that I'd been at the end of our European tour. Sure, once in a while I could reach a dehydrated ninety-five by refusing liquids for a couple of days and taking water pills, but that wasn't true weight loss. I'd had it with this crazy fight. Now that warm weather was coming, I could get out and walk, escape from the kitchen, my mother, and food. I was positive I could lose at least five pounds, maybe more.

My thoughts had been turning in space, but suddenly, almost as though she'd been tracking me, Kimmy asked, "How do you go about losing a lot of weight?"

Immediately on the defensive, I stammered, "But you certainly don't need to lose any!" Beautiful Kimmy, the princess of Glenridge, wanting to diet? It was absurd. She was perfect as she was. Being thin was *my* claim to fame. Along with modeling it was all I had to mark me as special. I was damned if I'd help her steal my title. "How much do you weigh?" I attempted to sound kind and understanding with the old friend. She had, after all, come to me as the expert.

She looked downcast, and shuffled her feet a ways before replying, "One hundred and twelve."

"But how tall are you?" I had to have height to evaluate weight. One hundred and twelve at five feet would be a bit chubby, and I could see the point in reducing. Of course Kimmy was neither that short nor the least bit overweight, but who was I to judge—my opinion of my own body reversed from moment to moment, and my view of the people around me shifted from fat to thin accordingly. It was like constantly drifting through a maze of funhouse mirrors.

"I'm five three," Kimmy responded, and waited for my verdict.

Where she'd unearthed this trust in me I couldn't imagine, but I was starting to enjoy this role as her mentor. I would have to be honest, but wily enough to dissuade her from any drastic reductions. I had enough competition as it was, from people like Candy and the waif in my algebra class.

It was true, however, that I would not like to weigh that much at her height, or even at my own. It wasn't so much the look of it but the sound of the numbers that jangled my sensibilities. I couldn't very well lie and tell her that she was too skinny to diet, because the fact was that I weighed less and measured taller than she, and I still considered myself fat. Nor could I pretend that I didn't know how she might go about losing, because she had known me when I was thirty pounds heavier. Obviously I knew what you had to do. But I was so ashamed of my eating habits. I could never tell her what I really did. Should I tell her just to balance her diet, or to go on one of the restricted regimes and just eat fish or fruit or vegetables? The carbohydrate plan? The low-calorie discipline? Sure, I'd probably tried every diet ever written, but there was no fixed method that worked. In order to lose, you just had to be obsessed. Mind over matter, as they say. You basically had to stop eating, and learn what to do to cancel the damage if, occasionally, you gave in to temptation. But to structure your own life according to this credo was one thing. To advise someone else was quite another. It sounded so rigid! I wasn't that compulsive. True, I still listed my caloric intake every day, and weighed myself sometimes twenty or thirty times, but was I a fanatic? I felt guilty whenever I overate, but I should. Indulgence was a despicable thing. Dieting, as far as I was concerned, was like a contest between good (abstinence) and evil (indulgence). If I followed through with the game, I'd purify myself. As long as I continued to eat in my wanton manner, I was tainted. But there was more to this than metaphorical warfare. The contest served a more mundane purpose. It distracted me from problems like the future, my parents' marriage, men, and all the other questions over which I had absolutely no control. I could dream about having an effect on people, about making a difference in the world, but at age sixteen, living at home with Mommy and Daddy, what could I really do? I was impatient and impotent, and dieting was like a security blanket that offered immediate gratification when I felt otherwise weak and powerless. But how would Kimmy understand this?

"It's not that I think I'm fat, exactly." She began spontaneously to explain her query. "But my weight is a big part of this image everybody has of me. It goes together with these hiphugger skirts and Pappagallo shoes." She disdainfully flicked a finger at her clothing. "In junior high it was wonderful to be popular. It was unthinkable that anyone would want out of the mold. The challenge wasn't to be different, but to fit into the trends as perfectly as possible. I don't know. Of course I'm still friends with all the same people, but I've been dying lately to make a big change, to cut away and do something that they don't expect of me. I'm not really sure what I'm talking about. Maybe it doesn't even have to be noticeable to anyone but me, but I've got to take some sort of control of my life. I'm sick of being the spoiled little rich girl who supposedly has everything and doesn't know the meaning of pain. That's a suffocating role to play! I look at you going off on your own, working in New York. You've found a way to get out of here. And I really admire the way you lost all that weight. I mean, I never thought you were fat or anything, but it must have taken such willpower and . . . well, a kind of courage. You aren't under the influence of people who tell you how 'healthy' you've got to look. Oh, no, I don't mean that you look unhealthy, either, but you know what I'm trying to say. You don't exactly come off as a lady wrestler. And nobody elects you for stupid roles like sophomore princess, either. I hated that so much. Some privilege!" She stopped, and looked at me with frustration.

I was astonished at this sudden outpouring. She and I had been leading such opposite lives for the last few years—or so I'd thought—and yet we'd developed such similar attitudes and needs. To think that she admired me!

"It's a little hard for me to fully identify with what you're telling me," I said. "I've always been one of your so-called followers. I would have chosen your popularity over modeling any day. And as for all the dieting, if I'd looked as good when I began that as you do, I never would have kept it up—but I looked disgusting, so I kept at it. Dieting has become a habit, a constant game. In a way, it's a kind of consolation for the fact that I've never been as successful as you. And I don't think I ever will be."

So we had a mutual admiration society. How nice.

Kimmy squinted at me, as if she suspected some underhanded motive behind my words. "Are you keeping trade secrets?" she demanded.

"What do you mean?"

"You act as though you don't want anyone to come near you, to know you. And you seem to resent compliments. Don't you like yourself?"

"Listen, Kim. You've just finished telling me all about how you sometimes hate yourself. Give me the same prerogative, hunh? We may have different reasons to question ourselves, in some respects, but it looks like we're basically pretty much alike. We're both spoiled Glenridge brats." I laughed briefly. It wasn't really funny. "Besides, there are no secrets to keep, as far as losing weight is concerned. The best way is to fast. Cold turkey. Water and water."

She looked a little offended at my reprisal and disappointed at the information I'd imparted. "Do you fast a lot?"

"It was easier when I first started to diet," I told her. "In eighth grade I was good as gold. But then I got into binging. All one day, nothing at all the next. It's a lopsided way to live, but it's like an addiction. I wish I could snap out of it. I keep vowing to go on, like, a week-long fast, but so far I haven't been able to pull one off. Of course, even if I had all the self-control in the world it would be hard, because my parents expect me to eat dinner with them every night, and also, they've been giving me a lot of grief in the last year or so about being, in their opinion, too skinny. . . . What would your parents say if you lost a lot of weight? And what about Johnny?" I'd never had to consider what a boyfriend would say to my ups and downs, but Kimmy and her football player had been together long enough that I imagined his response could influence her.

"Well, my parents are having their own problems these days. I don't think they'd pay much attention, one way or another. And Johnny and I may not be together much longer either. Oh, he's a sweetheart and all, but he's not tuned in to where I want to be. It's like he's part of the image I'm trying to get rid of. I've got to move out and do something completely on my own, without regard for what anyone else says or thinks. You understand?"

I nodded absently. Given her attitude, I would expect that Kimmy was thinking of leaving Johnny, but the news about her parents stunned me. They were upstanding members of the Glenridge community, one of the immutable couples. Her father an extremely wealthy advertising executive, her mother a gray-haired sprite of a lady, they seemed wed forever. At their home I had never heard a raised voice, never the whisper of argument. Kimmy's mother was a staunch liberal, president of the League of Women Voters, chairwoman of the Democratic Women's Club. Her father, like mine, spent most of his time in the city and had little to do with local affairs, but to my knowledge had always supported his wife's pursuits. It seemed odd, but I didn't explore the topic with Kimmy. Perhaps to outsiders my parents' marriage appeared idyllic too. Perhaps the only difference between Kimmy and me lay in our perspectives.

"Do you think of yourself as beautiful?" I asked her.

She tugged at a stray wisp of hair. It reminded me of white gold. The girl looked like a goddess. "I suppose it's inevitable, since everybody keeps telling me I am. And sometimes, like when I go shopping and stare at myself in a dressing room mirror or something, I really impress myself. But other times, early in the morning, or after I've been studying for a midterm, I feel like a total turn-off." Kim wished she were a better student. She was bright, not brilliant. "With me, that's something that changes constantly. If my self-esteem is up, chances are I think I'm gorgeous. I've been awfully dissatisfied with myself lately, though, and consequently I've been hating the way I look. Why, don't you consider yourself pretty?"

"Funny that it's such a sticky issue, isn't it?" I hedged the question, just as she had. "Modeling has sort of warped my perspective, I think. To be honest, I guess I went into the business to prove to myself that I was worth looking at. Not to seem like a crybaby, but I was always such a loser socially at school, I never could quite understand compliments when they came, you know, from adults or my brother and his friends. If I'd been popular like you, I doubt I would have even thought of modeling."

"Oh, you'd be surprised," Kimmy retaliated, "how little confidence that kind of attention gives you. Everybody stares at you all the time, but no one ever *talks* to you. They talk *at* you. They all think you've got life made—the old bowl-of-cherries story, you know? I mean, I feel guilty if it seems like there's a problem, or if I feel down. You can't complain, ever, because you have no right to. You have to uphold this image of innocence and perfection, or they'll treat you like a traitor. Honestly, half the time I feel like a prisoner.... The neat thing about you is that you cut out and created a life beyond all this petty bullshit."

The vehemence of her protest startled me. I glanced into her eyes, to make sure she wasn't playacting. They were like cats' eyes, flaming and icy at the same time, glowing green.

"Believe me, my situation is no better than yours," I said softly. I had at least to try to set her straight, but I wasn't at all sure I was up to the task. "All I've managed to do is to find new and different ways to disappoint myself. I don't feel that I belong in New York any more than I do here, so I dabble on the edges of both scenes, and constantly feel like a freak—only not a rebel, not a strong, beautiful eccentric. Just a misfit. In the city I'm too young, too naive to feel comfortable with the other models and photographers. I'm too stupid to handle the men on the streets, and the come-ons of the business. And worst of all, I can't even make enough money to make it worthwhile. There are all sorts of excuses—I'm not blond, tall, or American, or on the other hand, I'm not Oriental enough either. The few jobs I do get are a kick, admittedly, but it's a real schizophrenic kind of existence. You walk out of one studio feeling like garbage, and walk into another to hear them praising you like some sort of rare doll. I keep telling myself that there's more to me than my looks, but sometimes it's almost impossible to believe it."

"How does your weight fit into the picture?" Kimmy asked. "I mean, does it make you feel better about yourself if you don't eat? Or do you eat to reward yourself?" It wasn't a serious question. She knew perfectly well how I'd respond, but I told her anyway.

"I loathe myself when I eat. The only time I ever feel proud of myself is when my stomach is totally empty, when I climb on the scale and see that I've lost a pound—or two, or three, or four. When I eat I become an automaton. It's as though my subconscious takes over to punish me. I know. It's very weird." I felt as though I'd exposed an open wound, self-inflicted. It embarrassed me, and I hurriedly changed the subject.

"What I said about fasting, though . . . it's wrong. Just because I'm too weak-willed to do it any other way, you really should diet sensibly. Cut down, not out, as the experts say. You have to eat to stay healthy. Even as much fasting as I've done, I've really screwed up my body." Kimmy looked at me curiously. "I haven't had a period in three years."

"What does your doctor say?" she asked. "Has he told you it's because of your weight?"

"No. He says he has no idea what's wrong with me. Last year he ran me through a whole battery of tests and X-rays. They took pints of blood. Ugh! That was especially bad because the veins in my arms are so tiny that they kept missing, shoving the needle in over and over. And after it was all over they said they couldn't find a thing wrong. It's fine with me, actually. My mother keeps wailing and worrying, but as long as the doctor tells her I'm okay, what can she do!"

"I wouldn't mind having that problem. I can't stand periods. It seems so unfair that girls have to go through all that nuisance, when boys get away scot-free, doesn't it? I mean, if I wanted to have kids, I could justify it, but I have the maternal instinct of a rock."

"Funny. I don't ever want to have kids, either."

"But you've found a way out," she said pointedly. I supposed I had, in a way.

We reached the end of Brookfield Lane. Kimmy turned here. I went straight. It was still difficult for me to believe that she had approached me for advice, or that what I had said would have any effect on her. Despite everything she had told me, I found it inconceivable that she should want out of her spotlight position. She was the queen bee, the jewel of the community. To think that she even remotely identified with me! I would be interested to see whether she changed or remained the same.

We saw little of each other during the remainder of that spring. In the summer I devoted myself exclusively to modeling and solitary walks. True to my vow, I began again to lose weight and, as a consequence, most of my bookings. I was actually too small to fit the clothes my clients wanted photographed. But our conversation haunted me, kept reminding me of the spiritual significance of losing weight, of discipline, of sacrifice. Even at the expense of my modeling career, I was determined to keep reducing. It strengthened the soul, so to speak. In a way it made me a little smug to think that I was actually thinner than the average model. I had always considered myself much fatter than the norm, and still, inside, felt that I was. It was an odd kind of tug-of-war now. I wrote in my diary:

> I weighed under ninety-five again this morning. It really feels strange at times. I'm skinny one minute, fat the next. I should know better than to weigh myself every five minutes! I wonder if I'm not quite right, staring into mirrors and seriously thinking, "You are actually very beautiful." What's strange is that I feel almost sure of my near perfection, but that makes me feel so guilty. I must restrain myself, not eat, not eat, not *eat!* It's so hard, when you look at yourself and argue that you're thin enough, to keep down to five hundred calories.

But at the end of the summer and the beginning of school I realized that I had a long way to go before I reached "thin enough." Kimmy this time, not I, was the guide.

It was the second day of senior year. The school had moved into a new building, a concrete and glass extravaganza designed to accommodate the two thousand members of the student population who, for a decade too long, had been pressed into the cramped and deteriorating quarters of the old high school. We were all out of our element here. There were none of the army green lockers and prisonlike stairwells. The new school was built on the principle of openness and movement. No windows, no doors, but rooms with sliding walls that opened them one into another. Instead of waxed linoleum on the floors, we now had wall-to-wall carpeting. Instead of the old cafeteria, we now had a mammoth student center. Special wings extended from this central hub to allow for scientific study, the arts, administrative offices, and a school library. And looking outside during the "modules" allotted for lunch, we could see forests, ponds, and grass instead of parking lots and street. Tennis courts, a track, and the football field were tucked on the other side of a massive indoor swimming pool. It was this year's showplace for Glenridge, and it was exciting for us as seniors. But it was very large, and took a while for us all to adjust to. In the new environment even best friends looked a little like strangers to each other. Kimmy's altered appearance, however, had nothing to do with the change of scenery.

I first passed her on my way into French class. I did not stop to say hello. It was too difficult for me to handle my immediate reactions, and I hurried on before she noticed me. She had not only beaten me at my own game, she had sent me entirely out of the running. She had turned from golden to gray, from athlete to wraith. She must have lost at least thirty pounds, I figured as I nervously settled down for class. But she had not only altered her appearance She had changed the way she dressed, the way she moved, the way she smiled. She wasn't the artistic type, certainly, but now she reminded me of Candy. Her change in disposition was that extreme. It would be impossible ever to call Kimmy a freak or a slob, but she had done her best to strip away all vestiges of chic. She had given up hiphuggers all right, and adopted baggy coveralls, dark pullovers, and desert boots. Her skin, though summer-tanned, seemed curiously translucent. She wore not a trace of makeup, and her eyes seemed to have sunken, her mouth widened, and her nose sharpened. She looked as though at any minute she might burst into tears. I couldn't concentrate on class for the unsettled emotions the sight of her had churned up.

I couldn't tell whether I was reacting out of competition, guilt, or anger. Surely I couldn't nail myself with responsibility for her transformation. Surely I didn't envy her sickly cast. Or did I? I could pretend that I thought she looked horrible, that such self-destruction appalled me. I could tell myself that her metamorphosis had nothing to do with me, but the truth was that it fascinated and challenged me to follow suit.

I wondered how her new image would affect her popularity. She had, over the summer, broken up with Johnny. (Her parents hadn't, and never would be, divorced.) But would she continue to hang out with the same old crowd, or would she pull to a new direction? Coming out onto the balcony overlooking the student center, I spotted her in the crowd below. Instantly I could tell the trend her social life was taking. Her circle no longer consisted of linebackers and student government presidents, but it was nonetheless impressive. She now floated in the midst of intellectual musclemen: the editor of the literary magazine, the school expert on marine biology, political activists, and champions for civil rights. They wore shaggy hair, blue jeans, and expressions of intensity. They were all brilliant, handsome and, so it looked from where I stood, they all worshiped Kimmy. Standing next to me were two members of the soccer team who muttered something about how she looked like a skinned rabbit, but clearly the boys in her new entourage would not have agreed with them. Neither did I.

I wanted to know how she had accomplished this miracle, but I could not bring myself to approach her to find out. Now that she'd bettered me on my own turf, I considered her a kind of enemy. I would not go to her directly to find out her secrets, for I couldn't trust her to tell me the truth, but I would indirectly spy on her via mutual friends.

The girls she chose as confidantes under the new regime were all ebulliently healthy and hearty. I suspect that Kimmy was as skitterish about me as I was about her, for I threatened her supremacy as much as she had mine. But neither of us had any qualms about befriending those who obviously would never participate in our competition. They thought we were making a mistake to wrap ourselves so tightly into the pursuit of thinness, but they liked us despite our fetish. Dee was one such acquaintance, and it was to her that I addressed my questions about Kimmy's dietary habits.

I had ridden my bicycle to her house in back-country Glenridge, a distance of about fifteen miles, and we spent a good hour packing a picnic to take with us to the beach, another ride of twenty miles. Dee, an exuberant redhead ·with a lust for the forbidden and exotic, had an unrestrained appetite for food, as she did for life, and we packed a sizable ration of fruit, cheese, raw vegetables, and yogurt for each of us. I struggled with myself for a while to decide whether or not I should allow myself to eat today, and finally decided that after thirty-five miles of biking I could suffer a little sustenance. Once the decision was made, I even began to look forward to our feast. After all, I thought cockily, I had outdone myself with exercise (riding through back-country Glenridge is like riding a roller-coaster track). I wondered if Kimmy had whittled herself away through exercise or starvation.

"Have you ever asked Kimmy how she lost all that weight?" I hollered at Dee as we paced each other along the straightaway of North Street. I felt sure she knew. Dee was the kind of person everyone told secrets to. I had told her most of mine, and I assumed Kimmy had done likewise.

We stopped at a red light before turning down the hill toward Stanwich Road. "She refuses to talk about it," she informed me. "I heard somewhere that she ate nothing all last summer but Tab and carrots. That sounds kind of far-fetched to me, but . . . she sure did lose a lot, didn't she?" Her voice trailed off as she looked at me, then glanced down at her own muscular thigh. Dee was a large girl of the Isadora Duncan genre, not fat, but gloriously evident. It was inconceivable that she would ever diet, but at that moment there passed across her face a shadow that I thought I recognized as regret. The last thing I needed was another contestant. It would have been wise to change the subject, but I had to probe just a bit deeper.

"Hasn't she ever said anything to you about why she did it? Really. I'm curious how anybody could do that to herself. You two are so close. Surely she must have said something." I could feel my foot pushing its way down my throat.

Dee turned to start down the hill, but before heading off she looked straight at me and said, in a cold, clear voice, "You're the one who told her how. What are you asking me for? Self-discipline, remember? Cold turkey? What's the mystery?" And she zoomed on ahead of me.

We postponed further conversation until we arrived at the beach. My head throbbed from her (as I had taken it) reprimand. It was the first time I'd ever felt uncomfortable with Dee, and I felt it was entirely my fault. Why had I been so stupid? I should have known she'd side with Kimmy, should have kept my mouth shut.

We rode out to the end of Todd's Point, past the lagoon and the boat basin, around to the barbecue area that overlooks the Sound. Dee propped her bike against the tree and went to sit on a boulder by the sand. I lugged the packs off our bikes and settled down on the lawn. The discussion had effectively killed my appetite, but I was determined to eat anyway. When I turned down food it was for my own reasons, not because I was bullied into it. I would not let anyone else influence my eating patterns. My mind had been made up, and I would follow through. I would eat.

"Hey! You want some food?" I called to the girl on the rocks.

She turned and shrugged at me. Her voice, when she spoke, sounded perfectly friendly and normal. "I'm not really hungry. You go ahead."

I was immediately livid. There was no call for this. I clenched my fists in an attempt to control my peculiar rage. It welled up inside of me like an inferno, turning my blood to molten lava. Control yourself, I whispered, this is an absurd thing to get upset about. There's no law that says you have to eat with somebody else. Some people eat alone all the time. Some people would rather eat a whole pie themselves than share it. Why do you need so desperately to turn this into a social event? Either just take a piece of fruit and forget about it, or go ahead and skip it too. You aren't hungry. You're not chained to the decision to eat, you know. Why not count this as a blessing, an unexpected reprieve from extra calories? But the fire burned on.

I wasn't afraid that Dee would start dieting. That wasn't the problem. She wasn't built to be small, even if she did stop eating. She had powerful muscles and heavy bones. She was a dancer and an outdoor girl, and she enjoyed eating too much ever to give it up. And maybe most important of all, she was involved in too many other projects and dreams to dwell on calorie counting and exercise. She was what you'd call a well-balanced human being. No, I wasn't afraid of her; I was afraid of myself. I could not account for this surging tempest inside of me. If I'd taken a bite I would have gagged on it. It wasn't Dee's doing. She had no idea what was going on in my mind. I was my own monster, as usual.

I went over to join her. She smiled peacefully and pointed at a group of seagulls circling and diving into a school of fish. It was the end of September, and soon the weather would turn cold. Soon we wouldn't be able to come down here without heavy sweaters and coats. I should have been relishing these last drops of warmth, but instead I felt the oncoming chill. The inner fire had died, leaving in its stead frigid gusts of resentment and confusion. They would not let me relax. I hated . . . something? Someone? Myself?

Around the bend in the road, across the front pasture screams my mother's cocktail chatter. The Matthews, our nearest neighbors, are throwing a patio party. Above everyone else's, my mother's voice carries the quarter mile back to me. It claws at me through the open living room window. It sounds heavy and shrill, an insistent siren demanding my attention. I rise from the couch where I have been trying to read and turn up the stereo to obliterate her noise. I half hope it is loud enough to reach across to the party as a signal in response to her: Can you never restrain yourself, can you never see the dangerous power you wield?

My music is the soundtrack from the movie Z. The Greek rhythm lifts me to my feet, compels me to dance. I push back the living room furniture to make way for movement and, keeping an eye out for my parents' return, begin to improvise. I feel light tonight, and agile. It is a temptation to direct my energy to the kitchen. As soon as they walked out the door I felt the urge to binge, but I refuse to succumb, and dancing helps both to distract me and to fill the time.

I won't eat, I won't, I won't! When they come home I'll tell them I made myself supper. They'll never find the chicken wing I buried in the garbage. I'll tell them I ate that and the potato salad that I gave to the dog. And the coffee cake that I also fed to the dog after I'd picked the raisins out of it. They'll leave me alone then, and not make me eat supper with them. I'll just tell them I got too hungry to wait.

I lunge and wriggle across the floor and shake my shoulders

in time with the music. How lovely it must be to live in a place where whole families join to laugh and dance together.

If I skip dinner tonight it will make two days that I have gone without a meal. I am hungry, but I will wait. I'll survive at least until tomorrow. It hasn't actually been a fast, anyhow. I've had a few strawberries, and those raisins, and a couple of spoonfuls of yogurt. About four hundred calories since the day before yesterday. Not too bad, but not perfect, either.

I jump up and clap my hands above my head, reach down to touch my toes, whirl around, and sidestep into a fall. Energy, discipline, my own power will keep me going—psychic fuel. I need nothing and no one else, and I will prove it. Dropping to the floor, I roll. My tailbone crunches on the hard wood. My ankles clatter, but, caught up by the Greek beat and the sensation of freedom, I feel no pain. I will be master of my body, if nothing else, I vow.

But I can hear my parents' laughter at the head of the driveway, and so I quickly jump up, turn off the record, and scamper back downstairs to my basement hideaway. I do my dancing in secret.

"I was over at Candy's the other day," Carol told me as she stirred up the frosting for a carrot cake she had just taken out of the oven. "We were working on the layout for the *Glen Red*." She tasted a fingerful of the frosting, and made a face. Not enough sugar.

"Oh?" I responded. I rarely saw Candy, though I too worked on the magazine. I was on the editorial staff, she was an artist. I still stood in awe of Candy. She had become even skinnier over the past two years, and although she had a much smaller following than Kimmy, the two of them had received about the same amount of attention on account of their emaciation. People told me that I was skinny too, but nobody ever seemed to worry about me the way they did about them. I wasn't in their category. Strange though. We all had the same friends, and we all, through them, kept tabs on each other. "How's she doing?" I asked.

Carol stood quiet for a moment, her expression puzzled. She, like Dee, inspired feelings of comfort and trust. She would make an ideal mother, I often thought as I watched her cooking, sewing, painting, sculpting, or, as now, giving her complete attention to sticky questions.

"She keeps going. She works constantly, and everything she produces is lovely. But I'm sure one of these days she's not going to be able to make it through." Gently, she laid down her spoon, turned off the burner, and removed the saucepan from the stove. A clock in the hallway chimed four times. I had ridden my bike out at one o'clock (Carol lived a mile farther away from me than Dee). Soon I ought to be on my way, but it was always hard to leave Carol. She had a soothing effect on me. She was one of those people born wise. She never judged, but her opinions reflected the truth in a benevolently neutral way.

She turned and leaned on the countertop, and looked at me from beneath the overhanging cabinets. I was sitting at the long picnic table in the dining area of her kitchen. It was usually like this whenever I visited Carol. She was always involved in some project or other, always refused to stop what she was doing, but never minded company while she worked. I could never get over her candor and ease. She had a way of making strangers (though I hoped she considered me more than that) feel like very special friends. That was how she looked at me now—as if we were bosom buddies.

"Aimee," she said softly—I appreciated the way she used

my name when she spoke to me. It made me feel included, somehow, in her private world, her personal club—"she behaves like a slave, cowering under a whip. If she doesn't perform she'll be punished. Only there's no one pushing her but herself." She paused and gave me a quizzical glance. She knew little of my personal habits. Our friendship was based on classtime, mutual acquaintances, and visits like this one—chats fitted in betwixt and between. She was closer by far, I suspected, to Candy than she was to me.

"We worked from five in the afternoon until two in the morning," she continued. "At about eight we stopped for supper. Candy's parents had gone out for dinner, and her brothers had eaten earlier and gone to the library, so we had to fend for ourselves. Candy told me the family rarely ate together anymore, they all had such diverse schedules. So I was curious to see how she cooked. You know, in two years, this was the first time I'd seen her eat anything. She always claims she's not hungry or has just eaten or something. But I was starving, and I guess she felt sorry for me, because we stopped and she cooked some lentils and made a salad and brewed some camomile tea. That was fine, a little spartan maybe, but all right with me. Only when she served herself, I realized that I was eating at least twice as much as she was, which is not to say that I was stuffing myself, but she was eating virtually nothing. About a quarter of a cup of lentils, a few leaves of lettuce with vinegar—no oil, just vinegar—and the tea, without honey or anything. I made the mistake of asking for some regular salad dressing, and Candy looked as though I were a criminal. She found me some oil, but made such an awful face as she passed it to me. 'I just can't handle anything that heavy,' she answered when I asked her why she used only vinegar. I'm sorry, but I could never do that to myself. I mean, I can understand drinking it straight. I do that." I started at that. I too drank it straight. It was a dietary tactic that I'd never figured out, but whether it worked or not, it was unpleasant enough that it felt like it should, so I continued to subscribe to it. But Carol? She never dieted, and besides, she struck me as a kind of flower that would wilt if treated to such acidity.

"Why do *you* drink vinegar?" I demanded, breaking into her story. I tried to look bewildered, but the expression on my face betrayed me. She smiled benignly and shrugged.

"You know." She always knew what I did and didn't know. She was like a good witch, an omniscient protectress. "It's a digestive aid, of sorts. An internal ablution."

"Yeah," I admitted. "I drink it too." I felt that confession was in order, somehow. I felt that if I didn't make that point clear, I would lose credits toward membership in the club.

"But to drink it straight," she continued, "is a different thing from ruining salad with it. On the one hand it's a pleasant medicine, a hygienic aid like mouthwash. But you don't put mouthwash on romaine and arugula, do you?" She set the bottom layer of the cake on a plate in front of her and began to frost it. "It was really sort of painful to listen to Candy's philosophy about food. She's so obsessed, determined to deprive herself, to cut everything down to a bare minimum. But she herself is about down to the minimum, it seems to me. It's time for her to quit, but she's got her values so twisted that I think it may be impossible for her to recognize when it's time to start building herself back up. A couple of times I've tried to suggest that she might do better work if she weren't starving herself, but that just gets her back up. She insists that she's never hungry. I joke that she's as scrawny as a newborn colt—something a little more appealing than the standard plucked chicken—and she scoffs and tells me that she wishes she were really

thin. I wonder, I really wonder what she means by that. Aimee"
—again that conspiratorial direct address—"if I were eating as
little as she is I'd be keeling over, but she goes on and on."

I was beginning to feel uncomfortable. It was time to
change the subject, but Carol continued.

"Of course, Candy's mother is a nurse." Yes, I remembered
from visiting Candy's house when we were little girls. Her
mother was another of those impeccable women. She reminded me a little of Kimmy's mother, gray-haired and fragile. She
kept her house so squeaky clean that you felt ashamed to touch
the faucets in the bathroom. It was downright sterile, and
reeked, in a way, of Candy's mother even when she wasn't
home. Candy, to my knowledge, had never uttered a word of
complaint against her mother. "Although I've never asked
Candy what her parents think about her losing so much, I'm
sure they're concerned. Maybe they're just hoping she'll come
to her senses. But she's so bony. . . ."

"Haven't you ever wanted to be really skinny?" The only
effect this conversation was having on me was to make me
intensely jealous of Candy.

"Slender, yes, but I don't really mind myself the way I am.
And I could certainly never do to myself what she has done!"
Carol carefully tiered the second layer of cake. "It's got
nothing to do with looks. I just enjoy my body too much to
hurt it that way. Yes, I like myself too much." She followed
that comment with silence.

Yes, that is the difference between us, I thought. You have
such an endless capacity for pleasure. I honestly take pride in
pain. My, how melodramatic! Wisdom versus folly. Life versus
death. Light versus darkness. Health versus disease. I felt that
the tightrope was jiggling beneath me.

Candy poised further out on the rope. She had such a

delicate sense of balance that she could withstand every tremor, but I flailed wildly and looked to the platforms on either end. They were heaped high like cornucopias with fruits and flowers. Carol and Dee waved, urging me to give up and come join them in safety. Bathed in the colors reflecting from the food, they looked so enticing, but I hung on. (The endurance hang was the only physical fitness test I could ever do well.) I looked over my shoulder at Candy, and beyond her to Kimmy. They jeered at me, and glanced cynically to the ground below. Our mothers were holding nets beneath us, lest we fall or leap, but we had no assurance that the nets were strong enough to hold us—we were pretty heavy—or that they would hang on long and hard enough to save us.

"I should go." Carol's parents would be home soon, and I hated confrontations. Hers was one of those tightly woven families that played together, laughed, ate, and sang together. I could just see them all lining up to teach one another Greek dance steps. Carol and her father were extremely close. She and her mother got along quite well. She and her sisters adored one another, and with merry abandon exchanged all the delicious intimacies of their respective lives. I found it hard to deal with all that familiarity and sharing. Besides, I had a long ride home.

Carol finished icing the cake and set it under a glass bell on the dining room sideboard. Then she came with me to the front door and watched me mount my bike, my beloved ten-speed Raleigh, my pet steed. She picked up one of her four kittens as it scampered across the veranda and kissed its nose. Carol reminded me, as she stood there, of a maiden in one of the Tuscan frescoes I'd seen that summer in Europe. She was as delicate and soft and demure, and looked as though she'd endure forever. She hadn't a vengeful bone in her body, but her will was of steel so strong she never had to test it.

"Take care of yourself," she called after me as the gravel of her drive spun beneath my wheels. I think she believed that I would.

"It's sheer insanity, that's what it is!" My mother carved ink zigzags into the legal pad in front of her as she talked on the phone. She hadn't heard me come in. "Aimee does exactly the same thing. Mm-hmm. Makes you feel like a felon if you offer her a cookie, insists that she's never hungry, and tells you how she's had huge feasts everywhere else so that she never has to eat a bit at home. I know it. It's getting to be an epidemic, I think, this Twiggy craze. That little brat should have been given a good spanking and a hot meal and sent into a hospital, but instead she's made a fortune convincing our kids to starve themselves. Well, actually that's not true. Aimee did drum this thing up herself, before we'd ever heard of Twiggy, but the reinforcement certainly hasn't helped matters any. You go over to the high school today, and it's like walking into a concentration camp. I don't know what to do. Has anything you've told Barbara cut any ice? No, I know. It seems like they're never satisfied, and there's no way to convince them. How long has Barb been at this?" Mom was talking to Jane Callahan, an old friend of hers whose daughter, or so I'd heard, had been living for months on nothing but six eggs a day. Barbara attended Glenridge Academy, and I didn't really know her, but her younger sister, Beth, was in my class at the high school and had told me that Barbara, at five-eight, now weighed about eighty pounds. If that were true, she had even Kimmy beat. Out of view of my mother, I stood at the bottom of the steps in the living room and continued to eavesdrop.

"Fifty pounds in five months! Oh, my God! Have you tried to reason with her, or taken her to a doctor? No, it's true, it doesn't seem to make any difference to them. Betty Talbot has the same problem, I understand. She was talking about it at the Democratic Women's luncheon last Thursday. Her daughter, Liz, has been dropping weight nonstop for the last year. She was just a little bit of a thing to begin with, and now she's about the size of a sparrow. Betty was talking about having the child put into analysis. That seems an extreme measure to me. Really, it's all so absurd. That little girl is two years younger than Aimee. What a way for these kids to destroy themselves! And of course you know about Kimmy Sanders, don't you? That absolutely gorgeous girl, what a tragedy. No, there's no accounting for it. All you can do is hope that one day soon they'll snap to their senses. I, for one, have no faith in doctors or psychiatrists. They surely don't know anything more about our children than we do. I'm sure it's just a phase, anyway; a reaction, I think, to all the pressures of growing up today. The sexual freedom especially. Thank God we don't have to go through that now, hmm? I think it must be terribly hard to figure things out, with the kinds of expectations there are now. Our generation had no choice about getting our act together, did we. You either had to sink or swim, and that was that. We couldn't afford to sit back and contemplate our navels. Of course, these girls aren't lazy or anything, but it is a kind of luxury, or a reaction to luxury, that they starve themselves. Too much freedom? Christ, it's too much for me to figure out. I've got to go. It's time to think about supper." She laughed. "I know, maybe we can pull together some crusts of bread to go with the water tonight!" She sighed. "I wish it were just a joke. Oh, well. Thanks for calling, Jane. I'll see you tomorrow. Twelve, at the Pinetum Garden Center, right? Bye."

I tiptoed over and opened and slammed the front door to make her think that I'd just come in.

"Hi, Mom!" I cried gaily as I passed the kitchen. She was reaching into the freezer, but looked up and smiled.

"Would you eat a pork chop tonight?" she asked sweetly. "I'll take one out to thaw for you." The notion didn't begin to tempt me.

"Mother, will you lay off? I'll make my own dinner. Just forget it. Worry about you and Daddy." Feeling somehow like a trapped rat, I glanced around the kitchen. On the counter lay a white box tied with string. Dessert from the St. Moritz Bakery. I moaned and fled for my room. What would I do without this blessed sanctuary?

Behind me the pans began to clatter and the doors to crash. No words, no curses, just violent thrusts.

I shut the door at the bottom of the stairs and turned on my radio to drown out my mother's wrath. I pulled out my diary, unlocked it, and went into the bathroom. It helped sometimes to look at myself in the mirror when I needed sympathy and strength. I wrote:

Why does Mom have to care so much what I do, how I eat, how I dress, what I think. I have absolutely no self-reliance or independence. She's got her own life and her own ideas. They're fine for *her*, but why won't she leave me be to make my own decisions. Damnit! If I want to be thin, it's my body to treat as I please. Why won't she just stay out of it! Sometimes, the worst is, I start to listen to her, to think that maybe she has a point, but that makes me even more miserable. Then I'm wrong, and all the conviction I've built about the way I want to lead my life, the whole value system I'm trying to establish begins to crumble, and I feel that I have no right to exist at all. *Damn!* I wish I could find *me*, not just *her* daughter, but purely and simply me. Oh, Jesus. I feel as though I'm standing in the middle of a whirlwind. Hopeless and still. I want so badly to be a functioning individual on solid ground of my own. *Hell!*

Chapter Five

Triad

"Excuse me, but weren't you in my African Studies class last year?"

I looked up from my book into eyes that burned.

"You sat in the third row from the front. I sat in the back, by the window. Miss Harper's, fifth bloc, Tuesday, Wednesday, and Friday. That's right, isn't it?" He shifted on his toes and fingered the pages of the book he was holding. *Mein Kampf.*

I did recognize him, though we had never spoken and I couldn't remember his name. I nodded and smiled tentatively, terrified that I would blow this chance and send him scurrying away from me. For he attracted me in some queer, but powerful way. It wasn't that he was so good-looking, though he had a fair, sensitive face. It was more the way he looked into me. He seemed to see me, to know me inside out. He mirrored my intensity.

"My name is Ken Webster, if you've forgotten." He laughed softly and gave a comic bow of introduction intended to set me at my ease. It didn't.

"I'm sorry," I said, immediately apologetic. "That was such a huge class, I felt like I never knew anyone. But yes, now that you mention it, I do remember seeing you. You sat next to Chuck Grey, didn't you?" Chuck had been one of the senior loudmouths last year. Everyone knew and liked him for his outspoken wit, and I had often thought that his clique looked like one of the friendlier ones at Glenridge High. I assumed that Ken belonged to it.

"Yeah, and Angie Morley sat across the aisle from us, and Pat Gallagher sat behind me, but so what?" He grinned enticingly. "They all called you a snob. Aloof, to put it kindly. I was curious what you'd say if you knew that. . . . I mean," he hurriedly qualified himself, "I never thought of you like that, not that it makes any difference what anyone thinks, of course. But I had a feeling you had other reasons for acting so distant, and I always sort of admired you more because you kept to yourself. I guess I'm making quite an ass of myself. I really didn't mean to insult you. . . ."

I was thunderstruck. "A snob? Aloof!" I gulped, and stared at my bitten fingernails. I should make an effort to keep them filed and polished, they looked so awful. It was hot in here. Barely the end of October and already they'd turned the heat up full blast. . . . I wrenched my attention back to the fore. "I never realized anybody even noticed me. Certainly not any of you. You guys always came and went like such a tight-knit group. You had your own discussion groups, and worked together on projects and everything." A twinge of anger suddenly exploded in the midst of the hurt. "What was I supposed to do, anyhow? Stand up on a desk and sing the national anthem? I figured you'd give me the shaft immediately if I ever said boo to any of you. A snob! I just didn't want to humiliate myself, that's all." It seemed such a terrible injustice.

"Oh, I didn't mean it that way," he cooed. "They used to joke, but it was never anything against you. We all heard that you were a model, and naturally we assumed that you had bigger and better things to do than waste your time with the jerks in your African Studies class. I honestly didn't mean to insult you. It's just that—well, it was a stupid idea, but I just wanted to talk to you. Pretty lousy come-on, hunh?" He stopped abruptly and bent down to retie the laces of his desert boots. Everything about him seemed little. He wore jeans of brushed denim in a weird violet hue. They danced stiffly about his ankles because they were too short, but otherwise far too big for him. As was his shirt, which ballooned over his belt at the waist. It was hard to tell, but I suspected he was very skinny.

He straightened up, faced front, and asked if I'd like a ride home. I struggled to keep myself from gloating, from jumping too quickly into something I had no reason to trust.

"I'd love one."

"Are you ready to go now, or have you more work to do?"

I had been planning to stay another two hours, and then walk home, but I lied. "No, I'm finished. Just let me check out these books and we can leave."

"What are you reading?" he asked as I collected my pile. *Metamorphosis, Women in Love, Children of the Albatross.* "Fodder for the semester's independent study for humanities," I explained. "I want to spend as little time as possible in class." One of the joys of our "progressive" curriculum was that it allowed us so-called honors students to create our own programs of study, which allowed us to work on our own time and excused us from daily classes in humanities. We just had to confer with Mr. Sutter every couple of weeks and turn in papers at regular intervals.

"I'm doing the same thing," Ken nodded and waved his own tome. "But I'm restricting myself to one topic: Hitler."

I shuddered inadvertently and scooted around him to the chair where I'd dropped my coat. Hitler was not one of my all-time heroes. "If you don't mind my asking, why do you want to devote an entire semester to the villain of the century?" Now, now, give the boy the benefit of the doubt. Try not to make rash judgments.

He lifted his head, straightened his shoulders, and answered me directly. "I think it's important to learn as much about the horror that he created as we can. The terror, the suffering, the hold he had over, in a way, the entire world. It would be too easy for us simply to dismiss it as past history. I can't do that. I need to know about what went on, why he behaved the way he did, how he got away with it. He was an extreme man. It was an extreme situation. Extreme things fascinate me." He set his book down for a moment and buttoned up his blue-jean jacket. There was a long rip in the left side, extending from armpit to waist. "Obviously I don't admire the man, but there must have been some reason why he was able to grab such incredible control of people's minds and souls. He had a crazy kind of power, you've got to admit."

"Of course. But what good does it do to dwell on it? It seems like such a morbid fascination."

"To tell you the truth, I'm not exactly sure what my notives are, but it's not something I can brush off. I'm not Jewish, but I feel as personally affected by the holocaust as if I were. I have that personal kind of horror of Hitler. I know it sounds like a macabre obsession, but I keep trying to figure out what about the man, what kind of charisma or sadism, gave him the power that he had. I can't help it. I get a lot of flak on account of it, from teachers and friends. I'd love to be able to say what it is about old Adolf that keeps me coming back for more—maybe it has something to do with living in Glenridge, so completely removed from any such horror or threat. I mean, it worried me how upset I was by the movie *Night and Fog*. I was upset because of my own innocence and naiveté, and I decided then and there to open my eyes to what had happened and what could happen, even if it is unpleasant."

I flashed on scenes from the movie, which I too had seen in French class the week before. Heaps of dismembered skeletons. Lamp shades of stretched human skin. Mountains of hair shorn from the victims of gas chambers. Bulldozers plowing through mass graves. Little children roaming aimlessly, their eyes empty holes, their limbs like matchsticks, their naked bellies distended from malnutrition. I had reacted to the film as I had to the slides of Biafra; I was haunted, aghast, and tempted to examine the images over and over again. What was the monster, the demon, the god that could wreak such horror? What would it feel like to suffer so? How could anyone justify the difference between my experience and that of the victims in the pictures?

"I think I understand your point of view," I said, and moved across the room to check out my books.

"You're doing some pretty heavy reading yourself," he commented as we left the building and headed across the parking lot. "Kafka, Lawrence, Nin. That's not what I'd call a joy ride." It came out sounding more like a compliment than an insult. Why must I always take every motion, every word as a judgment pro or con? Why could I never relax and just talk naturally?

I affected a casual air and replied, "I've never had much use for joy rides. They seem like a waste of time. I mean, nothing really valuable comes easy. You know?"

He clutched his books to his chest and cringed under a sudden gust of wind. I could hear his teeth chatter momentarily. "I like you for saying that," he stammered. "It frightens me a little, because I agree so totally. But it makes me want to know you better."

I swooned. A warm shiver of pleasure shot up my spine, and my tongue tied itself in knots. I transferred all the passion from the pages of *Women in Love* onto the shoulders of my companion. In a matter of minutes he had won himself the title of my beloved, my confidant, my everything. I was convinced that we would fall madly in love with each other, would spend every moment together, would trust and depend on each other. The romantic in me ignored the cynic who warned that it would never work.

"If that's what you'd like," I finally answered, "we'll have to work at it. It sounds like a great idea to me."

"It seems to me that Ken treats you like a China doll," says Nan as she climbs from branch to branch. In the courtyard outside the auditorium there grows a giant oak tree that has this fall become our favorite hiding place. We come out here during study blocs and disappear high in the sky to discuss such issues as life, death, war, and love. Nan and I have been best friends for a month. We are both frustrated rebels who love to intellectualize and dissect our lives.

"A China doll?" I imagine a miniature head in porcelain— exotic, slant-eyed, untouchable. "Me? Why do you say that?"

"Well, you're so fragile, with your tiny bones and delicate features. How could he help but treat you as a doll?" She flattens herself against the limb above me and presses her cheek against the bark of the tree. The crimson leaves halo her face, and each time she exhales, a film of smoke issues from her lips. I wonder if I love her.

"Is that the way you think of me?"

"We have a different kind of relationship, Aimee. Don't be silly. Of course I'm not going to put you on a pedestal, the way I suspect he might. But there is something about you that impresses me. It has to do with your intensity, I think, as well as the way you look. But the fact that you *are* so tiny in itself gives an indication of what I'm talking about—it's like you've got more important things to think about and do than eating. That's a dumb simplification, naturally, but you do make that impression. It's like, since there's so little of you physically, there has to be more spiritually and intellectually. You're different, you know. And I'm so fed up with most of the other kids in this school. I feel as though I can connect with you in a way I can't possibly with all the cheerleaders and Ladybug look-alikes."

"But what about people like Dee and Carol, and Kimmy Sanders? That whole crowd feels pretty much the same way we do." I am a little confused by the compliments Nan is showering on me. I don't believe I deserve the acclaim.

"You're better friends with them than I am," she admits. "I would like to get to know Dee and Carol better. I probably would like them. Kimmy, on the other hand, I don't trust. She didn't have to destroy herself so theatrically. It happened too obviously and too suddenly, and I think she only did it to attract attention, as if she didn't have enough already. Maybe I'm not being fair, but I can't see what she was trying to prove by losing all that weight. She did change her image to one I like more, but she's still got her elite little circle around her. Oh, I don't know her very well, like I say. I'm probably just jealous."

She climbs down to sit next to me. We dangle our legs and

stare silently into the glassed-in corridor that leads from the student center to the auditorium. Inside a group of sophomore girls practice cheers for this afternoon's cheerleading tryouts.

What changes we all go through! I can remember when I would have given anything to be a cheerleader, when my own wardrobe consisted primarily of Ladybugs and John Meyer outfits. Now I sneer at competitive sports and wear Levis to school. And I can remember Nan when she was too meek to answer when called on in class. She was at Eastern with me, though I hardly knew her name then. She was another A student, but unlike me, she seemed content to huddle in the background instead of proving her "leadership qualities." She participated in no after-school activities, never ran for student government. She even looked like a mouse. She used to dress in gray cardigan sweaters, which she buttoned up the front, and brown tweed skirts. She always came to class impeccably neat, her hair cleanly cut to chin length and held back from her face by a tortoiseshell headband. The band matched the frames of her glasses. When she took the glasses off you could see her enormous eyes, which looked perpetually about to tear up, though I never actually saw her cry. She never let anyone know how she felt or what she thought, and I remember wondering if she had any friends at all.

I steal a glance at her and smile. She now wears steel-rimmed glasses that don't hide her face. She wears no makeup, and her hair is long and pulled back into a ponytail. She no longer looks like a stereotypical bookworm—she looks like an exceptionally clean-cut hippy. She's exchanged her tweeds and cardigans for fishermen's-knit pullovers and man-tailored jeans, and instead of looking like a frightened fawn she now wears the expression of an enlightened skeptic. She reads *The Greening of America*, *The Second Sex*, and Plato. They are not on our humanities reading list, and she's not even doing a related independent study project; she just wants to read them for her own information. That's one thing I admire about her.

Another thing is her calm. She leans back in the crook of the tree, pulls a giant leaf from a branch at her side, and holds it up to the light. It is flecked with scarlet, magenta, and gold. It looks like a palm of jewels as she turns it in the sunshine. Infinite patience, that's what I see in her good-natured face. She has a look of the madonna, secretive and wise. She hasn't Dee's exuberance or Carol's gentle dynamism, but Nan looks— well, everlasting and ageless. Self-sufficient. She doesn't wear her intensity like a flag around her neck the way I do. I wish she could teach me how to relax.

The bell rings, sounding the end of our freedom. Nan has physics now. I have oceanography. We walk together to the science department, and I notice how much taller she is than I am. Almost two inches. She's built like a boy, and walks with a long, low-slung gait. As we pass an ashtray she clumsily lights up a Marlboro and drops the match among the wads of chewing gum, candy wrappers, and cigarette butts left by the lunchtime hordes. I shudder. The sight nauseates me, and I ask Nan how she can bear to smoke, knowing how bad it is for her. She replies that it gives her something to do with her hands. I glance down at my own shredded fingernails. Six of one, half a dozen of another, I suppose. But Nan looks so awkward and stiff smoking. She holds her cigarette like a joint of grass, between her thumb and the tip of her forefinger. Just for a second she looks to me as though she's a patchwork of other people's habits and attitudes, and I wonder if perhaps she's not quite as tightly woven as I've imagined her. That's a sudden, fleeting impression, however, which vanishes as soon as she smiles goodbye.

Diary entry:
Oct. 22, 1970

I've just heard myself spoken on the radio. It is almost midnight, and I feel lonely and raw. WNEW broadcast a poem that exactly spelled out my mood. It spoke of the crying need for compassion and sensitivity, the need that hides behind the icy masks we all wear to protect our independence. I have that problem, so much more than I even am aware. Despite myself I appear to people "aloof" and unattainable. I warn them away from me at the same time that I wish they would come closer and help me to figure myself out. Even those who do come near—Nan and Ken especially—know only the facades of composure and false strength. And I, likewise, see only the obvious in them. These mutual admiration societies are farcical!

And so, frustrated, I destroy myself in quantities of food. It's such a meaningless existence, and yet, so all-encompassing. How I love to destroy myself, to make myself so fat, so fat that I loathe myself. What a miserable cycle! It keeps me occupied, that's for sure, and distracts me from my own basic ineptitude. But I get so disgusted with the constant self-centering.

There are glimpses of something more worthwhile when I get away from home. If I'm alone, and moving, and haven't eaten, then I feel good about myself and can see the world in a way that I think must be normal. Sometimes it happens in New York that I'll walk down the street and feel totally alive. I can dive in and become part of the puzzle, and it's actually fun. There the world seems to consist of intertwining movable pieces, one of which is me. There is so much to see, so much that is constantly new that it's like a liberation from all the petty junk inside me. I can almost get away from the trap of my hunger, my schedule, my emotions, my damned compulsions. Oh, God, how I despise myself for being so weak! I wish I could get out of my body entirely and fly!

My mother stands on one side of the kitchen and whips up a soufflé to go with the veal chops she and my father are having for dinner. I stand on the other side of the kitchen and dice the eggplant I'm going to steam for myself. I've become a vegetarian this week. It's a development that annoys my parents, but as a result of it we have reached a tentative solution to the dinnertime diet contest. I will eat with them, but prepare myself a completely separate meal. That way I need not sabotage their food. I can keep accurate track of my intake of fat, carbohydrates, and calories without getting on their nerves, and they can eat whatever they want without threatening me. Of course they still insist on offering me a slice of meat here, a dollop of whipped cream there, but I remain adamant and vicious in my refusal, and gradually they let up on me. They want us to be pals.

"Who's been giving you a ride home the past few days?" my mother asks. She sounds enthusiastic and interested. I'm not particularly eager for her to meet Ken, however. As soon as she meets him she's bound to express an opinion of him and I doubt that it will be positive. He's not her clean-cut, beautiful sophisticate, and I expect her to raise myriad reservations about him. When she does, I know her argument will sway me, no matter how hard I try to hold my ground. So I hedge the question, distort the facts, and fit my description to her desires.

"A guy named Ken Webster," I tell her. "He was in my African Studies class last year. He's an artist, and very smart." I bring out as many of his credentials as I can think of immediately.

"What kind of artist?" she asks obligingly. I cringe at the thought of the calories in the heavy cream she's folding into her soufflé.

"He paints and draws, primarily. He was on the art staff of the *Glen Red*, and as part of Homecoming, he's getting a five-hundred-dollar prize for a drawing he did of Jimi Hendrix. It's from the Old Glenridge Art Society." I smile proudly. The prize will be awarded at assembly on Friday afternoon. Then that night we'll go together to the Sadie Hawkins dance. It will be the first dance I've ever attended with my own "boy-friend."

"I'm impressed," she concedes. "What's he planning to do with his art?" Always the same question. What are your goals? Where will you go from here? How well are you preparing for the future? There are acceptable channels, you know, and total wastes of time. Be careful! Be careful! Do you want to be an ambassador, a diplomat, or a scholar? If he's got so much talent, how do you know he'll use it properly? I wince, trying to think of the appropriate answer, and work to contain my annoyance.

"Well, to begin with, he wants to go to Yale. It's got one of the best art departments in the country, and he's got the grade-point average and the SAT scores to get in." Ken and I are both in the National Honor Society at school. We've both scored in the seven hundreds on our College Boards. But Ken knows what he wants to do with his life—he has a passion. I have nothing. How can I impress my mother with his vast superiority to me?

"You could get in too, if you want to." Somehow, the way she speaks, she seems to condemn rather than laud me. Or is it me? Why do I take everything my mother says as an accusation?

"Maybe. But I don't have any reason to particularly want to go there," I bleat. "I'm not sure whether I want to go somewhere that's known for its English program, or somewhere that specializes in international affairs. I just don't know what I want to do. That's what's so great about Ken. He knows what he wants and is going after it. I mean, he can't tell you how much money he'll be earning ten years from now, or whether he'll be living in a palace or a slum, but at least he's got his work. That's enough, as far as I'm concerned. He's way beyond me!" My voice rings in my ears. I drop the last syllable abruptly and bend to my chopping.

"Darling!" My mother syrups her voice. "I didn't mean any harm. I'm not pushing you anywhere. As far as I'm concerned you're just marvelous the way you are. You don't even have to go to college if you don't want to. I'm proud of you, that's all, and I hate to see you praising somebody else at your own expense. You have all the cards in your hand. You can deal any one you please, and the chances are you'll do well." She wraps her arms around me and kisses my hair. I won't turn around, won't look at her. If she can't see how she hurts me, I won't give her the satisfaction of my telling her.

"But what if I never figure out which card I want to choose," I spit, and shiver out of her grip.

Behind me, I can tell, she's backing away, cold and resentful. I hear her spatula grating against the side of the mixing bowl, the clank of metal as she turns her soufflé into a pan, and then the crash of the oven door.

"If you can't figure that out," she lashes back, "it's your privilege, but don't blame me!" She hurls the spatula into the sink and stomps to the back of the house.

She's right, of course. She's not to blame. It's my own problem if I'm not strong enough to stand up for myself, if I haven't enough confidence to legislate my future. And maybe Ken's just a distraction. What's Mom trying to tell me? Does she think I'm going to imitate him? That I'll draw his card instead of thinking for myself, and then regret it? Oh, why do I care so much what she thinks, and why does she hassle me all the time? I get so exhausted with all the constant second-guessing!

Four o'clock in the morning. We crept down the driveway and pulled up back outside the entrance to my room. The house was dark, no parents waiting up, thank God. Ken switched off the motor, reached over, and stroked my hair.

"Do you want to come in for a second?" I asked. It had been such a wonderful night, I couldn't bear to see him leave.

"Of course I'd love to, but there's just not enough time. I still have to pack, and we leave for the airport at six." He and his parents were flying to California for his older brother's wedding this weekend.

"I can't believe you're really going to pull this off. Do you enjoy these endurance tests?" I played with his fingers as I spoke. He had thin, rather bony hands, so pale they seemed almost to glow in the darkness. There was something a little ethereal about Ken, both physically and spiritually. He had a penchant for performing superhuman feats. This weekend, for instance, he had set himself the goal of going four days without sleep. He made excuses about how he wanted to go to the Sadie Hawkins dance with me, and to the after parties, which we'd just come from. And he insisted that he couldn't sleep on the plane, and that, as best man, he'd have no chance to sleep before the wedding. So he'd decided that he would take advantage of this occasion to test himself, that now, even if he did have a chance to sleep at some point, he wouldn't.

"Why do you want to do this to yourself?" I demanded.

"You understand. Don't give me this mothering," he joked. "Finding your limits, pushing yourself to extremes, we've discussed this before. Don't play the voice of reason with me, little girl. You've got the very same streak of insanity yourself."

It was true that we'd discussed this before. It was, in fact, practically all we ever talked about. It had started with Hitler and the idea of suffering and pain, but had expanded into a more immediate comparison of our attitudes of self-worth, integrity, and individuality. I had explained to him my struggle with weight and indulgence. He had inspired me to become a vegetarian, and had told me how he fasted at least once a month, often for three or four days at a time. He said he did it as a method of cleansing and meditation. He made it seem so sane ... not for the sake of losing weight, but for— well, almost religious reasons. We had talked about exercise and again found common ground. Ken was no athlete, but he constantly set himself performance goals, like this going without sleep, or driving for hours without rest, or biking up steep hills in high gear. I had no doubt that he'd follow through on this weekend's scheme. He told me that he often stayed up all night, that he did his best artwork after midnight. He called himself a loner. Yes, we had a lot in common. Enough to make me jealous when he outdid me. He was so much more ambitious than I, so much more independent.

"I'm afraid I haven't nearly the energy you have, though," I said wistfully.

"Oh, yes you do. You just show it in different ways." He leant over and kissed me behind the ear. "I think that's why I love you."

I shuddered, unable to speak. What exactly did he mean by that? Love was an awesome word—emotion—concept. I read about it, I dreamed about it, I longed for it. But now, as the word rolled off Ken's tongue, it terrified me. It was different from the trust and affection I felt for Nan, different from the admiration I felt for Carol and Dee. No, this was potentially dangerous. It quivered with worry, envy, and fear. It was everything I'd ever wanted up to now, everything I'd thought I wanted, anyhow—love and tenderness—and yet at this moment it sent me into panic.

I held his face in my hands. I could barely see his eyes glistening like jet marbles, the pupils huge and round. His curly hair scraggled about his cheeks. His lips parted thick and soft in question at my hesitation.

"What's wrong?"

"Nothing. Nothing." I tried to disguise my sudden terror. "It's all happened so fast with you, that's all. Love is kind of a loaded word, you know? I don't really know what it means . . . we've been seeing each other less than a month. I'm sorry, it's just that it's going to take me a while to get used to it." I couldn't lie. Why was I so goddamn honest? It would have been so easy to go along with him. To finish this lovely night with vows of love—wouldn't that have made everything picture-perfect? Why did I have to go and ruin it! I thought of the tiny white lights flickering through the trees that had decorated the gym for the dance tonight. Paper flowers like magnificent snowflakes had bloomed at the edge of the dance floor. We had moved in slow circles, hugging each other tightly under a canopy of multicolored streamers. There was such comfort in his arms. We could have been on the Riviera, or in some Alpine valley, or deep in the jungles of South America. All evening long I had pretended that we were lovers—Audrey Hepburn and George Peppard running through thunderstorms together—but now that Ken wanted to turn the illusion to reality I cowered. I hadn't the courage to play this game.

As I knew he would, he turned away from me. He was hurt and surprised, and I regretted my words, but it was too late. He sat with his hands in his lap. I reached out and touched his shoulder, but he shook me away.

"I'm so sorry," I stammered. "I've never felt like this about anyone before, and I don't know how to act or what to say."

"There's no script," he snapped bitterly. "If you felt it, you wouldn't have any problem. It's all right. I'm a big boy. Just forget it." He sounded dismal, as though he would start any minute to cry. I felt helpless and guilty.

"Please," I tried, "don't be hurt. I hate to leave you this way. I honestly didn't mean that I don't love you. . . ." And then I gathered up my nerve. "I *do*." It sounded disgustingly feeble. I'd only made things worse.

"It's all right, I told you. You don't have to lie. I'm sure you didn't mean any insult. I'm just sorry if I offended you." He softened his voice. "Maybe I'm just tired. But I have a long way to go before I can wind down. Don't get upset. I'll probably see you in school next week. We'll see what happens."

I got out of the car, went around to his door, opened it, and leaned inside to kiss him good night. He was shaking. "Please, Ken. Don't." Who was I to comfort him? "I wish you wouldn't push yourself so hard."

"Look who's talking," he murmured, and put his arms around me. I felt him run his fingers up and down my spine. "Maybe we're too much alike. Maybe that's what you're afraid of. Maybe you're smarter than I am."

"If we weren't alike we wouldn't want each other, though."

"We'll see."

He kissed me lightly and closed the door.

In the morning, while Ken soars en route to Los Angeles, I

keep quiet in my basement room so that my parents will think I'm asleep and not ask that I join them for breakfast. I want neither food nor their questions about the dance. Was it fun, did you have a good time, how did you like it—how many ways can we find to ask you the same meaningless question? We want you to be normal, happy, healthy—here, have a sweet roll, and how about some eggs? No, no, no, I want to scream. Leave me alone! I don't know how it was, how I felt, what I want. And even if I did understand what's going on, I wouldn't share it with you. No, you can't bribe me with health and wellbeing, or false enthusiasms and concern. I won't be kept in the fold that way. I want so badly to fend for myself, and you make that impossible. Why can't you let me make my own decisions, fight my own wars, make my own mistakes! I'm sure you mean to make my life easier, but all that does is block me. Whose fault is it, yours or mine? Can't you see what the real battle is about? It isn't food. It isn't Ken. It's you and me, it's expectations and regrets. Yes, we're all conspirators against each other, unwittingly cruel. You pretend to be so proud of me, so happy that at last I have found a boyfriend. But you'll find fault with him when you meet. It's the same as everything else. You applaud as long as what I do conforms to your expectations, meets your standards. But the minute I begin to slip you get that disappointed look and whimper with worry and concern.

The clanging of dishes and pans signals the end of their morning meal. From the front of the house comes the roar of an engine. My mother must be going shopping. I sidle upstairs to tell my father that I'm going for a walk. He looks up from his paper to ask how the dance went. I tell him it was fun. He tells me that's nice, and lapses into silence. My mother is the chief interrogator around here; he still cannot talk to me. Just as well, I tell myself. Let him have his secrets, I'll keep mine, and never the twain shall meet.

He sits at the dining room table with the newspaper spread before him. He smokes cigarette after cigarette despite all protests from my mother and me that he's killing himself with nicotine. He bites his fingernails as badly as I do and drinks as much coffee. But sometimes, like this morning, he loads his with cream, and unless he goes to the thrift shop, he will sit here motionless until lunchtime. What a strange character. I wonder if, had I not listened to my mother's complaints all these years, I might be able to be friends with him. But that's a useless question. The pattern of our mutual detachment is irrevocable.

He looks up momentarily, and asks when I'll be back. And don't I want some toast or something before I go. Trying to hold back a surge of irrational anger, I answer that no, I don't want anything to eat, and I don't know when I'll be home. He shrugs and tells me to have a nice time, and I hurry out the door.

The morning twinkles with the crispy chill of late autumn. The leaves of the Japanese maple at the foot of the front steps flutter brazenly in juicy color of seasonal gore. Everywhere there is that feeling of intense life which immediately precedes death. The exuberant thrill of adrenalin before the final breath is drawn, and the leaves wither and fall. How I hate the winter and cold. But at least for a few more days I can still go out alone and walk. Later for hibernation.

I stride, pressing off with my toes and rolling forward heel first. It usually takes me a mile or so to establish a comfortable gait. Then gradually building up speed, I turn into a perpetual motion machine. It annoys me if people stop to ask if I want a ride. Why do they assume that I would want to take the easy way? How dare they interrupt my thoughts!

For the motion is one game, and thought is another that I play while stalking the wilds of Glenridge. The object of my mobile mind game is to probe beyond the mundane, to test myself to see whether I'm capable of digging deeper than the surface of daily affairs. I try to take the junk that clutters my head and sort through it and make some kind of discovery that could substantiate my behavior. I want to create a personal philosophy. Any problem can fit into this game.

Take Ken, for example. Since first meeting him I think about him more often than anything except food. So I begin with the assumption that my feelings for him reflect some nidden quality in myself. What do I expect to gain from our relationship? Ecstasy, or pain? Fantasy? So far all it's led to is an incredible load of guilt. Who would have guessed that I could hurt him? And how does that hurting make me feel? Awful. It has nothing to do with the companionship, trust, mutual respect I'd envisioned between us. Wrong. It has everything to do with it; it proves that there never was any trust or understanding, for if there had been he wouldn't have turned on me so quickly just for admitting the truth of my confusion.

But dig deeper.

I must have done something more wrong than simply stating the truth. There must be something about me that he dislikes, something that surfaced through my confession. It may be . . . that I'm too shallow to feel deeply, to commit myself. Yes, that's it. It gets back to the idea of extremes. Ironic, because that's exactly what I admire most about him: that he has the strength for commitment, to push and test himself, to prove his devotion. Yes, now I'm beginning to understand.

I take a breather. The road climbs steeply around the curve onto Cat Rock Road. The noon sky snaps with clear, frosty light. There isn't a cloud in sight.

Ken, devotional intensity, finding meaning and faith. In order to make him truly love me (put aside for the moment the question of my loving him), I must show that I deserve his love. The best way is to follow his example, to discipline myself, to equal him in stamina and determination. This is something important to work toward. It's not just my own stupid whim—it's about earning honor. In a way I suppose it's the same thing I've been saying for years, that abstinence is good and weakness evil, but through Ken's example I see things much more clearly. So I hereby resolve to limit myself more than ever in food, sleep, and imitative thought. I must make myself unique and powerful, must keep more to myself from now on, and search out my own borderlines.

I lunge forward and tighten my thigh muscles. The leg feels hard and strong to the touch, but when I relax and straighten, it feels flabby. I've got to work to turn my whole body to rock.

Okay. Now let's turn to the question of Mom and Dad. Deeper, deeper. Come on, you can analyze that one into perspective, can't you? For example, let's try to figure out why you burst into tears yesterday when you found the clipping about lady economists that she left on your desk. She was only trying to be helpful, you know. Just trying to spur your imagination about future possibilities. A likely story! What she was really doing, as usual, was trying to manipulate me, to steer me in her chosen direction. And what about Dad? He never says a word about stuff like that, certainly never gets on your back. No, but he supports her one hundred per cent, you can bet. Remember the days when I went into the UN with him, and he proudly announced to all his colleagues that his little daughter would grow up to be a lady ambassador, or president, or work for the State Department. You can do with your life whatever you please, they say, but they make no bones about what they'd like to see me do. Oh, they wouldn't disown me if I became a waitress or a secretary, but they sure would be disappointed. And that would be worse than the most brutal whipping they could give me.

I wonder what would happen if they pushed me off into the blue and forced me to make my own way. If the cords were severed I might have a chance to discover my real mettle, but as long as they stand so solid and watchful behind me, how can I possibly ignore their wishes? Oh, they keep saying they make no demands on me, that I lead a life I have selected for myself, but you know that's not really true. They are proud of me, aren't they? And don't I keep making sure that they are? I earn my own money for college, keep my room neat and clean, maintain honor grades. But if I slip up they're just as aware of it as I am. Even Dad has his insidious ways of keeping me in line. If, for instance, I get more B's than A's he's sure to make some remark. He pretends that he's kidding, but he doesn't fool me. The fact of the matter is that I ought to be perfect. I could be perfect if I'd just try harder, and whenever I let myself slide it disappoints everyone involved.

So what's the answer, kiddo?

I stoop to pick up a particularly spectacular leaf and proceed to tear it to shreds.

The answer is always the same: I have got to be harder on myself. I have got to eliminate the distractions.

Which brings us to food.

I heave a sigh, and break into a run, pumping as fast as I can the last mile to the junction between Cat Rock and Stanwich Road. I feel so angry with myself that I want to explode.

Food. That's the scourge. I can't get away from it. If I don't eat I gloat, but think constantly of what I'm missing. If I do eat, I damn myself, and over and over again count up all that I regret eating. But the thing that's truly unforgivable is the way it blinds me to the rest of life. It completely warps my sense of reason. . . . If only I could forget about it, take it or leave it as a child does, but no, I am obsessed with it, and there's no way out.

When, three hours later, I return home, my parents are dressing to go out to dinner. All the better for me, that I may go without food for another night. (I used excitement about the dance as an excuse last night to skip supper.) I can do an extensive set of calisthenics to pass the time instead.

Despite my efforts to slink unnoticed down to my room, my mother hears my footsteps and calls hello. I return the greeting and mutter something about having tons of work to do. That's not true, but I do not want to talk to her. I firmly close the door behind me as I enter my room, but within seconds, without knocking, she barges in anyway and begins the drill.

She wears a helmet of curlers, and smells heavily of talcum and Je Reviens perfume. Her bathrobe, an extravaganza of sable velour, regally sweeps the floor. As she invades I dash into the bathroom, and pray that she'll take the hint and leave. No such luck. She sits patiently on my bed and removes her nail polish while waiting for my account of the dance. I refuse to speak unless spoken to.

"Well, are you going to tell me about it or aren't you?" she asks brightly. She's oblivious to her violation of my territory. The whole house, after all, belongs to her.

"What would you like to know," I counter defensively.

"Everything, of course. How did he like your dress?" She who styled my costume now wants her handiwork applauded. "What was everyone else wearing? Where did he take you to dinner? What did you eat? What were the decorations like?

What did you do afterwards—you did get home a bit later than we expected, you know." She raises her eyebrow in challenge.

"It was all wonderful," I snarl impatiently. I have energy to run and jump, but none to spare for this pointless chatter.

"Oh, come on now, darling. Don't be like that," she pleads in that hurt, peevish tone she always uses to make me feel guilty.

But I won't tumble.

"There's nothing to tell, Mother! You've been to dances in your day. I'm sure this was just the same. A mess of high school kids all milling around in long dresses and dinner jackets. Some amateur decorations disguising a hot, smelly gym. And a lot of people too drunk or stoned to pay any attention to what's going on." Even Ken and I had our share of wine, but I won't mention that.

"Now really!" she laughs, unperturbed. "It can't have been all that glum. This Ken must have given you a hard time?"

"No," I snap. "That's not at all true! We had a fantastic time together."

That's just the opening she's been looking for.

"Well, tell me about him, then. Where did you go for dinner?"

"We skipped it."

"Honestly, Aimee! What do you mean you skipped it? Is he in on your demented diet scheme too?"

"Forget it, will you? It's no problem. We just weren't hungry. We were having too good a time."

"Doing what?" she growls. "Just what *were* you doing all that time that was so absorbing?"

"Talking," I insist, and turn on the radio very loud. "What does it matter to you what we do with our time, anyhow? I'm here perfectly safe and healthy and sound, aren't I? Or don't you trust me?"

"Darling, please don't accuse me like that. I do worry about you. It's not that I don't trust you, but you look so sort of *vulnerable*, and I don't know how this Ken feels about you. You are just so tiny that I'm afraid if anything were ever to happen—well, I just worry."

"Well, don't."

The Stones scream "Sympathy for the Devil," and my mother plugs her ears.

"Turn that thing down. Or off!" she orders me. Grudgingly, I do her bidding.

"I had a good time last night. Ken is now in California. And that, for the moment, is all there is to it. So what's the problem?"

"I don't know. What is?"

I sit down at my desk and open my notebook. For a moment I study the page intently, scanning my notes without comprehending a word. Then I turn to face her.

"Nothing," I answer, "except that I have an awful lot of work to do."

She gives me a razor-edged look and rises to leave the room.

"If you'd come to your senses and put some food into yourself you'd feel a lot better, and we might be able to improve communications around here."

I wait for the door to slam after her, then turn up the radio to full volume and hurl my books across the room.

"I just can't believe it's over so soon, Nan. It seemed so perfect, so beautiful. And now he's up and told me to get lost."

"I can't believe," she said gently, "that he meant to hurt you. Did he really say that?"

"Oh, not in those exact words. But that's what he meant."

"What excuse did he give?"

"He said he needs to be by himself more, that I'm too much like him, and we'll become dependent on each other if we stick together. He's probably right. He's much more level-headed than I am. But it hurts so badly, after all the hopes I'd built up."

We sat in silence then, inspecting the greasy spots on the formica tabletop. Across the restaurant a baby bawled, refusing to eat the spoonful of pancake its mother was holding to its mouth. They were the only other customers at the Post Road Pancake House this Wednesday afternoon.

"Have you ladies decided what you'd like?" The waitress had Goldilocks curls and an hourglass figure that strained the seams of her polyester uniform. She stopped smiling when she learned that we just wanted black coffee. She'd have to charge us each the minimum 75¢. That was fine with us, however, so she sashayed back between the booths to fill our bottomless pot.

"Well, did he say that it was you, specifically, or did he tell you he just wasn't going to go out with anyone right now?"

I watched the waitress coming down the aisle.

"He implied that he couldn't get involved with anybody. And that's all right. I can sort of understand, I guess. But I don't honestly believe it. I bet anything that he'll be seeing other girls. You know, I think I cut my own throat by acting so hesitant the night of the dance. What a fool! Why am I so stupid?"

"That is absurd, you know, to think that way," Nan reasoned with me. "What you told him was perfectly honest and direct. How could you be expected to fall at his feet after only a few weeks together? Just wait a little while. He'll come to his senses. Probably be back within a month. If that's what you want."

I burnt my tongue on a premature sip of coffee.

"What do you mean?" I lisped. "Why wouldn't I want him back?"

She fondled her mug and planned her response so as not to offend me. "Well," she began slowly, "on the one hand, you act like you're too much of a loner for such a tight relationship." I began to protest that I wasn't nearly as much of a loner as I seemed, but she shushed me and continued. "But on the other hand, I think you might expect more from him than he's capable of giving you. I really doubt that he's any stronger than you are—even though you treat him like a god. I can't predict how you'd behave if he did come back, but I have a feeling it would be very either/or. Either you'd freak very quickly and tell him you couldn't handle having him around all the time, or you'd cling to him until he ran away again. Don't get me wrong, Aimee. I'm as big on 'true love' as you are, but I went through exactly the same thing with Jed, even before my parents got into the picture. And I don't think I'm rationalizing to excuse their behavior; I don't think our relationship would have lasted, 'cause I was leaning on him way too hard."

Jed, Nan's new love, had been busted for possession of marijuana last week, the same day Ken had returned from California. And while Ken was telling me that he had to stop seeing me, Nan's parents were forbidding her to see Jed. We were both complying with orders. Another thing Nan and I had in common: We were both sickeningly obedient.

"You paint a pretty bleak picture," I complained. The steam spewed from the surface of the coffee, vanishing as it reached eye level.

Nan faked a laugh. "It's the age of the identity crisis."

"You aren't kidding."

"Maybe it's a passing phase."

"Maybe it's not."

Diary entry:
November 10, 1970

The only point now is to lose weight. To devote myself to that may distract me from the loss of Ken. And if I get skinny enough, maybe he'll feel guilty and come back to me. I kind of doubt that, though, because he's dropping weight himself, faster than I am. Last I heard he was down to 118, which for a boy with his bone structure is awfully thin. I am now ninety-two, up a pound from last week. It annoys the hell out of me the way I continue to eat despite all my promises. Yesterday I drowned myself in prunes, crackers, and diet soda. I ate until I felt like vomiting, but the worst of that was that when I tried to, I couldn't. If I'd just keep myself *out* of the kitchen I'd be all right, but it's as if there were a giant magnet in there. Mom and Dad aren't even so bad anymore, now that I've got them trained to let me stick with vegetables at dinner. No, I'm my own worst enemy. If I could just lose five or ten pounds by Thanksgiving I'd be satisfied. Then, once I was really thin, I might let myself eat food that was actually good for me. If I ate things like yogurt, cheese, and milk, maybe I wouldn't succumb so easily to junk food. At least Nan has gotten into fasting too, now. That should make it easier for me to stick to my guns. We are fasting together for the next three days, and having her monitor me will keep me from cheating. It's so stupid! But it's all I have to comfort me now, all that matters to me. Any other kind of happiness seems shallow and false.

"You know, it's amazing," said Nan, "I'm beginning to understand how she managed to lose all that weight." She was watching Kimmy race across the opposite side of the student center. It looked like Kim was still losing, too. Her blue jeans, which were French cut and meant to fit snug, bagged around her knees so that you could hardly believe that she had any legs at all beneath the fabric. It was almost the first time I had ever seen her all by herself.

"She sure has changed, hasn't she?" I thought of her triumphant reign as queen of the in-crowd at Eastern Junior High.

"Yes, but since we began this fast, I can see how it could happen." Nan and I were on the third day of abstinence. I had cheated twice, one time eating seven raisins, another having half a saltine. But Nan claimed that she hadn't had a thing except coffee since the beginning.

"You really like it, hunh?" I felt ashamed of cheating, but was basically pretty proud of myself for sticking it out. I did not, by any stretch of the imagination, enjoy the project, however. I thought even more about food than normal, and I found it almost impossible to concentrate on my schoolwork, which was a problem that had been bothering me more and more the past year but which increased whenever I stopped eating. So did my insomnia. Sure, I loved the feel of my pelvic bones jutting out, but I could not even pretend that I enjoyed the deprivation.

"I'm surprised how much I like it, yeah," Nan confessed. "It makes me feel so clean and free. You know, with my little brother and sister at home, my mother keeps all this junk food around the house, and we always have the stereotypical family meals, and I never even thought about doing anything like this before. Maybe it's just that it's a novelty, but I don't think so. For the first day I felt hungry, but now it's like gliding. It makes me feel good about myself. And I don't even want to eat when I smell or see it. Last night I baked bread and cookies until midnight, and I didn't take one taste. I can't explain it, because I've always eaten like a pig. But last night it was as though the mere smell filled me up." I thought of the days I had passed by Arnold's Bakery to smell the bread instead of eating lunch. "And the other thing that's neat is how much more energy I have. It seems as though all my senses have come alive."

I agreed with her on that. "I know. It's like you see things brighter, their outlines sharper, and their colors much more vivid. I guess I've been doing this for so long I'm not that sensitive to it anymore." (Old pro speaking here. Whom are you trying to kid?) "But I know that whenever I eat more than I should I can notice the difference in my perception. Everything dulls down. But I don't know about energy. I get pretty draggy when I don't eat. Although what's exciting is that when you start to eat again, you can practically feel the fuel shooting into your bloodstream. And if the first thing you eat is sugar, just a teaspoon or so, it's like shooting speed—or what I'd imagine speed is like, anyhow, I've never done it—but it gives you this explosive burst of energy that's great."

"I know you said that this was the only sure way to lose weight," she queried, "but you don't fast *all* the time. How do you keep from gaining when you don't fast?"

I knew I was showing off, but I couldn't see any harm in telling a few trade secrets to my best friend.

"Well, my parents are my biggest problem, because they keep trying to find ways to ram food down my throat without me realizing it. But if you pay acute attention to everything you eat as you're eating, you can both ignore them and keep track of your intake so there's no room for confusion. And the slower you eat the less it takes to make you feel full. Sometimes I feel stuffed after eating a few, say, brussels sprouts.

They're especially good, by the way, because you can take them leaf by leaf and make them last forever. They're like the little Japanese game balls we used to get for party favors when we were little, you remember? They had toys inside, and you had to unravel them to get the prizes. What a sucker I am for games! I ought to be four years old again, I swear." I took a breath, and grinned. It was fun to play the authority. With Kimmy and Candy and the others running around I was starting to feel like humpty-dumpty, but Nan assured me that I was just as thin as they were, which, though I didn't believe her, boosted my ego. "Once in Vienna, when I was fourteen, my parents bought me a tiny Sacher torte. It was about the size of a petit four, but I just took nibbles of it every day, and I think the thing lasted for over a week. I remember that Charlie did the same thing with his bar of chocolate in that children's book, *Charlie and the Chocolate Factory.* Do you remember reading that as a kid?"

Nan laughed at my nonsensical memory for detail.

Not detail, I retorted, it was food that had me hooked.

"But what," proposed Nan, "if you were around food all the time, cooking or serving or something? Don't you think you'd get sick of it? I mean, I started working at Friendly's Ice Cream Parlor last week, and already I feel as though if I never see another ice cream cone it'll be too soon."

"Wow, I didn't know you were doing that!" I was impressed. My parents would never approve my getting a job as a waitress, but it seemed so responsible. On the other hand, though, I would never trust myself to resist with that much food at my disposal. "No, I don't think I could survive at a job like that. I'd blow up like a blimp just by looking at all that ice cream, and they'd fire me within days!" I laughed pathetically. Nan didn't know how severe my eating sprees could be.

"I seriously doubt that you could ever resemble a blimp,"
she said coolly. I wondered why she hated me.

A warm breeze is blowing. In the near distance waves wash
the beach, and the cry of seagulls fills the air. It's nearly
sundown, and I am sitting by myself. I am not lonely.

The blanket under me forms a soft, clean carpet on which I
arrange my household of books and mirrors. I also have a pad
of paper and pen with which to list my passions. I wear
nothing but a tank suit, which gives my body a silky feel and
displays the contours of my hipbones and ribs. My hair falls
like a sheath about my shoulders. I pull it across my face, and
it becomes a curtain of russet highlights through which the
ocean flickers and blazes.

I flip back my hair, and turn my face to the sun. It bathes
me in a stream of warmth as comforting as a steamy shower. I
could stay immobile forever.

But I must work. Camus, says the jacket of the book at my
feet. *The Stranger*.

I open to the first page: "Mother died today."

For a second the beach burns magnificently, and I look up
to see a glittering jet screaming across the sky.

I turn to the last page:

For all to be accomplished, for me to feel less lonely, all that
remained to hope was that on the day of my execution there
would be a huge crowd of spectators and that they would greet
me with howls of execration.

I discover that I'm eating, but I can't see what. My arms are
swathed in gooseflesh, for the warm gusts have turned into a
wintry blast. My hand moves mechanically, but quickly, to
and from my lips. I chew and swallow great gulps , but cannot
taste them. My belly swells, begins to hurt, but I cannot stop. I

eat without utensils, and my fingers stream with grease. Mirrors on either side of me reflect expansive thighs and a blossoming bustline, but all I can see directly of my body is my feet. They look as though they're inflating, becoming red and grotesque. Next my hands and wrists come into focus. They as well seem like disgusting balloons, fleshy appendages. *"Chubby little girl"* sings a monstrous voice.

I look up to see Nan hovering above me.

"What are you doing here?" she demands scathingly. "Eating!"

I cannot keep my arm still. Hand to mouth, hand to mouth.

"You're supposed to be taking an exam," she informs me. "Right now. And you haven't even read the right book." She kicks sand on *The Stranger*.

I choke and retch, but nothing comes up. I look up at her helplessly, terrorized, unable to think or speak.

She turns her back and, laughing, runs off down the beach.

I woke shivering from the dream and grabbed for my bedside lamp. My stomach growled loudly. It felt as though the digestive juices would eat right through. When I got the light on I saw that it was four o'clock. Wide awake and too shaken to try to sleep again right away, I got up and went into the bathroom to weigh myself. Eighty-nine. That helped make the strain worthwhile.

It had taken me almost two hours to get to sleep in the first place, and then the nightmare had wakened me after less than an hour of rest. I had to do something to calm down. I had an exam in the morning, it was true, and I couldn't afford to stay up all night. Maybe some calisthenics would help.

I turned on the radio to WNEW, where Allison the Nightbird was playing the Birds. I began with toe touches. "To every thing, turn, turn, turn." And moved into double-time jumping jacks. "There is a season. Turn, turn, turn. And a time to every purpose, under heaven." Then down to the floor for some sit-ups and leg lifts. "A time to be born . . . a time to die."

I reached over and turned it off.

But still I couldn't get to sleep. Nor could I warm myself. There were three blankets on the bed, but I was freezing. I curled tightly into a ball and rubbed my feet. They were icy.

The exam was to be about D. H. Lawrence and his theory of love. Love as an omnipotent master. Homosexual versus heterosexual love. What could I possibly say about it all? After all the pages I'd stared at without knowing what in hell he was talking about. After all the fuss I'd made about how I *adored* Lawrence, thought he was a genius. I was a fraud.

I knew Mr. Sutter hated me. He saw straight through my act as few of my teachers could. He was like a firefly, flitting all over the school at a hundred miles an hour, always on, always interested in what his students were doing. And he always knew who was up to what. He was my adviser on Lawrence, and you could bet that he considered me the great pretender, and he was right. I didn't have the vaguest idea what I was talking about half the time. Because I was spending more attention on my goddamn stomach than on school.

What in hell is going to happen to me when I go to college and have to face real responsibility?

"I'd like to start seeing you again," said Ken. The phone line crackled, and I stared intently at my bleeding thumb. I'd just ripped the entire nail off.

"I can't stand talking over the phone," he said. "Could I come over?"

"Sure. But I don't want to stay here." My parents still had

not met Ken, and I was in no great rush to have them do so. They were out right now, but I didn't want to risk running into them later.

"Well, we could come back to my house, then." He waited.

"All right. Half an hour?"

"Sure. I'll be there. Bye."

"B'bye, Ken."

We had spoken no more than five times in the last three months. Christmas had come and gone in its usual fashion, with a cycle of binges and fasts, family parties, and this year a few pleasant evenings with Nan. But Ken hadn't even called to say hello. And since we had no classes together, and he spent most of his time in the art department, we almost never passed each other at school. So although I thought of him, wondered and worried about him, I had assumed that he'd forgotten me. I couldn't imagine what had prompted this comeback.

I waited at the front door for his arrival, and as soon as the battered VW reached the top of the driveway I ran out to meet it. The wet insult of early February penetrated straight through three layers of sweater and coat. My bones moaned and my teeth chattered as I clambered into the car.

Ken smiled. "I didn't know anyone else's teeth but mine did that."

Awkward and embarrassed, I told him I was sorry. Whenever speechless or confused, I always apologized.

We were silent as he backed the car around. Then he asked if I'd been going out with any other guys. I told him no, had he been seeing any other girls? He said no, and there was again an awkward silence.

"Well, what have you been doing for the last three months?" My voice had a disagreeable edge of bitterness to it.

"To tell you honestly, I've been doing a lot of thinking—and a lot of drugs." He let that sink into my puritanical mind for a few moments, then explained, "I've been trying to sort out exactly who I am and, among other things, whether I'm strong enough to support my end of a relationship. I have these terrible fits of depression, and people tell me that I think too much, that it's hard to be around me. I feel so close to you, but you are, if anything, even more intense than I am." It always startled me when people told me I was intense. "I don't know if it would be the healthiest thing for us to get back together . . . but I can't stop thinking about you. I want to see you again, and I do think I'm in better shape than I was last fall."

I was too stunned to experience pleasure or panic, and so chose to keep things going on a relatively impersonal level. "How have drugs helped you sort things out?" I tried to keep the judgmental bite out of the question. I didn't have much confidence in drugs.

"It's sort of difficult to explain if you've never done them, and of course different things affect different people different ways. I don't want you to get the idea that I'm a junkie or anything, but I was tripping at least once a week, and smoking grass or hash every day. That probably sounds to you like I was just spacing myself out, but it was actually important to help me get a perspective on things that were—well, starting to destroy me."

"What kind of things? You seemed okay when we were going out."

"I'm a terrific actor," he quipped, and thrust the VW into fourth going down North Street.

"Well, so what did you find out on all your magical mystery tours?" I could hear that nibble of disapproval again. What was wrong with me, anyhow? I was going to make him hate me because of some stupid prejudice that I didn't even believe in. If anything, I admired people who had the guts to use drugs. Face it, if my parents didn't stand so staunchly against them I'd surely have experimented myself. To tell the truth, the fact that Ken used them stood in his favor. Here was my surrogate rebel!

"Well, last fall I was feeling like there was no hope for me. I hate to make this sound like a sob story, but I felt as if I'd been stripped of any confidence, faith, that I'd ever had. I felt like the world was deteriorating around me. When I met you, my first reaction was to put all the pressure for my future on your shoulders. Whether you knew it or not, I was hoping that you'd provide me with a reason for living. God, it sounds so melodramatic, I know. But that's the way I was thinking. It was really a very good thing that you backed off like you did." I started to object that I'd made a terrible mistake, which he'd misunderstood. "No, I know you thought you didn't mean it, but the fact that you even hesitated was enough to throw me into a fit of despondency so bad that I knew it would be a mistake to put you through any further strain."

I wanted to tell him how much more damage he'd done by spurning me, but before I could think of a way to phrase it he'd gone on.

"I think I figured out what was behind that Hitler fixation. During one of my acid trips I looked in the mirror and saw myself as him. It horrified me, but not because of what he was—not because I was freaked at being that cruel or sadistic—but because I saw at that moment that there was some kind of real strength that he had that I didn't. You see, some part of me knew that the face I saw didn't belong to me, but that same part wished it did, because it was jealous of the internal power that I didn't have. It was as though by inversing things, by showing me myself as I wanted to be, I was able to see what I lacked. Do you understand?"

I nodded slowly, too frightened by his words to protest that I didn't really want to hear any more.

"But then, when I saw myself in that imaginary costume, the other side of me flew into action, and while I stood there a battle took place in the mirror between Hitler and me. We were, like, wrestling for control, and when I won Hitler vanished, and this other guy—who looked a lot more like me, but still wasn't exactly—this other guy shook his fist and grinned at me. He was telling me, I think, that I could make it, but I was going to have to fight against a lot of bad stuff inside and outside if I was going to make it to the top."

He stopped for breath. I pretended to take what he was saying in stride, but my real reaction was one of morbid fascination and, strangely, admiration.

"Another hurdle I had to get over," he continued, "was that I couldn't trust anything or anyone. Not my parents, not my friends, not my teachers, not you, and most of all, not myself. That's why I shut you out, but if you think I was mean to you you should have seen the way I treated my parents. Of course I hardly ever see my father, anyway"—Ken's father was vice-president of a large company in New York and, like my father, rarely came home before nine at night—"but as you'll see in a minute when we get to the house, it's very difficult to avoid my mother. She plants herself in front of the TV in the den, and you can rarely enter or leave the house without confronting her. But I managed simply to ignore her. It was so cruel and rude, and I knew she was hurt by it, but I couldn't act any other way." It was hard for me to imagine him treating anyone rudely. Even when telling me that we were through, he had apologized and absolved me of responsibility for the actions he was taking. He almost convinced me of my innocence.

"I came out of that phase," he said, "when I nearly flipped

out on a mescaline trip. I dropped late in the afternoon about a week before Christmas. It came on so gradually that for hours I thought the stuff was no good. But about midnight I started to feel like the walls were closing in. Did you read Poe's story 'The Pit and the Pendulum,' when you were little? It was just like that. I sat on the floor in the middle of my room, because I was afraid the bed would collapse on me. I couldn't even listen to music, because all the lyrics sounded like accusations against me. And I had to turn all my drawings face to the wall, they all looked like such trash to me. I've never felt so totally worthless and frightened. All the junk on my desk and bureau looked like weapons, and they seemed intent on harming me, so I cleaned them off into drawers—that was very weird, a lot like in Cocteau's film *Beauty and the Beast*, in the palace where all the tableware and furniture comes to life, remember?" I had just seen that movie in French class. Suddenly I could imagine what tripping must be like. How exotic! I wished that I had the nerve to try it.

"But things got stranger and stranger, and my terror kept intensifying until I just sat there clenching my fists, and praying that I'd get through to morning. I somehow felt that the light would release me when dawn came. If I closed my eyes I felt as if someone were standing over me with a knife, about to strike, so I kept my eyes open. But the climax came when I looked down at my own hands. At first it seemed as though they would turn into claws, or hammers, or something that could be used against me—that I would use against myself—but then they became beautiful instead. They were— well—likable. I don't know. They were soft and yet muscular, capable and sensitive. They were about *me*, and the sight of them reassured me that I was a good human being. When I looked up everything in the room was back in perspective. I turned the radio on, and the Beatles were singing 'Maybe I'm Amazed.'"

I smiled. The theme of the Sadie Hawkins Dance had been "Maybe I'm Amazed."

"I know. It's silly, isn't it?" Ken paused. "So then I took all the stuff out of the drawers, and everything was all right. It was incredible how relaxed I felt, and how confident. I got into bed and went to sleep, and when I woke up I still felt great. I talked to my parents before I went to school in the morning— it must have been the first time in weeks. They just about freaked, I think.... It must sound pretty pathetic to you that I could put so much stock in drugs, but I really do believe that they've helped me. And now, honestly, I don't need to keep doing them." He looked at me sheepishly. "Because I'm more interested in being with you."

This confession struck me dumb, but luckily we were just pulling up in front of his house, and I didn't have to make a response.

The Webster home was an unremarkable establishment, split-level, shingled, and spanking white. There was aluminum weatherstripping around every window, an automatic alarm detection device hooked up to every door, and a neatly landscaped flagstone path leading to the front door. It looked as if it had been cut out of my first-grade Dick and Jane book.

Ken led me through the screened-in back porch into the den where, as promised, his mother awaited us. But she had fallen asleep in front of *The Match Game*, and she didn't budge at our entrance. Ken put a finger to his lips and steered me toward a side door, and the stairs leading up to his room.

I was too embarrassed by the situation to stare openly, but I couldn't help stealing a glance at Mrs. Webster in passing. She appeared several years older than my own mother, and stouter. Her glasses, suspended from a chain around her neck, rested on an expansive bosom. She wore a beige shirtdress that looked as though it came from one of the several matronly but expensive dress stores that line Putnam Avenue in downtown Glenridge, and she wore her hair in a short, graying permanent that further accentuated her plainness.

I tried to sound sincere when I joined Ken at the top of the stairs. "I'm sorry she's asleep. I was anxious to meet her."

"Another time, I'm sure," he replied flatly.

His room sat above the garage, and overlooked the driveway. It had but a single window that let in just enough of the cold February light to powder the scene. Ken's drab navy and gray furnishings didn't help to brighten things. My mother would have hated everything about this place.

"Would you like to sit down?" He offered me my choice of a seat in the straight-backed wooden chair at his desk, a metal stool in front of his drawing board, or the bed. I sat stiffly on the bed and, leaning back a bit, rested my head on the ceiling which sloped down behind me.

"You still haven't fully explained why you want to start seeing me again," I prompted, to bring him out of his gloom and to get things back on an immediate track.

He paced the room a few times, apparently as nervous as I wasn't letting myself appear.

"I can't tell you how sorry I am for putting you through all that shit last fall," he blurted. "I knew what a mess I was from the beginning. I had no right to lay it all on you, and certainly not to expect you to solve the problems. But one thing, you gave me a goal to work toward. . . . Like I said, I'm still not sure whether it's a good idea or not, but I can't stop thinking about you. Increasingly the past few months I've realized what a fool I was to lose you. I won't blame you now if you tell me to beat it, but—well, I think we made too strong a connection to simply dismiss. You can call whatever terms you like—I'm not asking you to be my lover or anything. I just want to keep the lines of communication open, if you do."

Apparently distraught and afraid to confront me too quickly, he bent down to select a record from his collection on the floor beneath the window. With his white, lightly freckled complexion and high-strung expression, he was not quite handsome, but I saw in him a tortured beauty that drew me closer by the second. I felt so keenly his restless, striving spirit, his mistrust of the superficial, and yet there was also a craving for honesty that matched my own.

He put an album of Elton John on the turntable and set the volume low. The singer's halting moan poured across the room. His music sucked me in, filled me with romantic yearning that bordered on mawkishness, but it felt wonderful. I would become his slave, and he would become my mentor. We would be companions and confidants, supporting, and succoring each other for the rest of our lives. I was fully aware that an artificial atmosphere had made me its prey, but I warmed to the passion flow with enthusiasm, nevertheless. The time was right, the stage was set, and I noticed a wonderful subsidiary effect. My stomach grumbled with empty hopes, and I was too distracted to care.

It suddenly occurred to me that love might help me escape the tyranny of my eating compulsions, that in fact those compulsions were probably offshoots of loneliness and insecurity. All the stuffing and subsequent self-abuse had helped to pass time that should have been devoted to someone else. But now that Ken was ready to save me, I could normalize. I'd no longer feel the urge to binge because I'd devote that energy to him. I'd probably lose more weight than ever, and without struggling! It would be fun perhaps to cook for him, since I wouldn't even be tempted to eat. No, I couldn't imagine eating around him, not more than a few bites anyway—I had to keep my stomach flat so as not to be embarrassed if he touched me. Yes, I felt as though I would finally get a taste of freedom from the monster.

Elton hooted and hollered over the gushing of my fantasies. He sounded brutally cynical, but I tried to ignore him.

Ken leapt to the rescue. "I think you understand me, Aimee."

He used my name like bait, and I hurtled myself toward it. "I want to," I whispered melodramatically, "very badly."

He stood unsteadily in the middle of the room. The afternoon light sneaked in the window behind him to make a pale corona of his frizzy hair. He ruined it by sitting down.

He took the chair at the desk next to me and swiveled to face in my direction. He wore a thin cotton shirt pinstriped in ugly maroons and gray. It was open at the neck to reveal a patch of his chest with its translucent skin and skimpy growth of hair. I adored him, but I was certainly not physically attracted to him, and I hoped he meant what he'd said about my calling the shots on the relationship. Kissing and hugging were fine with me, but any further—well, it was out of the question. Sex—animal, filthy, debasing, ugh! No, it wasn't so much that Ken himself turned me off; I wouldn't be able to do that with anyone. Lucky that he was sensitive and gentle enough to understand, and let me have things my way.

Motionless, and apparently more relaxed now, he watched me go through my mental gyrations. My face must have undergone some enormous changes, for when at last my thoughts came to rest at grateful approval, he laughed and leaned forward to hear the verdict.

"You passed the test." I grinned. "Was it that obvious what was going on inside?"

He reached out and put his hand on my knee. "I told you, we think alike. Sometimes I'll watch myself in the mirror, and my face does exactly the same thing, phasing in and out, shifting gears at breakneck speeds. It's hell to do self-portraits. Maybe that's why I do so many of them, though."

"Do you have some here? I'd love to see your work, if you'll show it to me." I wasn't ready to have him touch me. This was a good stall tactic, and besides, it was about time that I became acquainted with *his* obsessions.

"Of course. Forgive the shambles. I'm not the world's greatest housekeeper."

I scanned the room. It wasn't antiseptic clean like the rest of the house, but it was excessively tidy.

"Oh, it looks all right on the surface," he explained, bending down to pull out some portfolios from beneath the bed. "But the way I live reflects the way I order my existence: You maintain appearances by piling the confusion under the bed. You just keep stuffing the chaos in the closets until they burst open. Then you're forced to roll up your sleeves and deal with the mess. You begin to throw the garbage out, and hope that you'll come across some forgotten trophies worth keeping. It's like taking inventory. But you're in trouble if all you come up with is crap. Then you get depressed and make promises to change, to organize and discipline yourself. I say I'm going to quit chucking everything to the back and hoping eventually to notice something worthwhile there. I vow to be more discriminating about what I take in in the first place. Upgrade the quality, in other words. But I find that I make such mistakes when I try to judge too quickly that I'm better off by taking in the junk, and at least having something to hope for, than by regretting something I was too stupid to appreciate, and lost. You see, when we were first going out, I had sort of decided to try the second approach. I'd cleaned out my closets, so to speak, found nothing there, and decided to sterilize my existence. That was why I gave you the heave-ho so fast when you didn't immediately behave as I wanted you to. You weren't that pristine little doll that would look so pretty on my dresser, nor were you my guardian angel, so I scratched you. I figured if I didn't take any confusion in, I wouldn't have to worry about throwing it out later, you see. But I got awfully tired of staring at all the empty shelves, so I began to stockpile again, cluttering up my life. And the more clutter there was, the more comfortable I felt, and finally I worked up enough nerve even to face you. I was fully expecting you to shoot me down, you know."

I'd gotten lost in the metaphor, but dimly realized that it had worked out in my favor, and smiled reassuringly. He seemed to think I was following him, and I wished I could, but taking in, throwing out—what exactly did he mean? I didn't dare expose my ignorance by asking questions, and so went as far as the notion of cleaning each other's closets from now on, or something along those lines. It sounded fine to me, and I sat on the floor beside him, surrounded by open portfolios of artwork, and felt relieved that the oration was over. The self-portraits gave me something tangible to work from.

"Has anyone ever called you conceited?" I joked. There were notebooks filled with his image. There were sardonic grimaces and pouts, severe stares and disquieting leers, piercing frowns and worried scowls, but not a single smile in the bunch. Apparently the medium made no difference, for there were works in pencil, ink, watercolor, and tempera, and in all the air of gravity predominated.

"Did no one ever teach you to laugh?" I asked after browsing through the stack.

It seemed I had overstepped my territory with that, however. He roughly snatched the notebook I was holding and told me that I'd probably prefer to look at the pictures he'd done from photographs. I attributed his gruffness to some quirk I would understand when we knew each other better, and looked as he directed me. He was right; I did think these drawings better than the first. They were, in fact, impressively slick.

"They're fantastic!" I oozed, trying subtly to compensate for my unwitting violation of his privacy. But at the same time I was inspired by these drawings. They were so crisp and professional. I wondered what it must be like to have such talent. Too afraid of possible failure, I had never tried to learn to draw, but now facing Ken's accomplishment, I became ambitious. I vowed that I would give it a try. To make him proud of me, I thought.

To prove that I was not inferior.

All the stars were there, in two-dimensional splendor and grace. Mick Jagger, Jim Morrison, several renderings of Dylan, Hendrix, George Harrison and Ravi Shankar, Frank Zappa, Richie Havens—they went on and on.

And then, at the bottom of the pile, Hitler hailed us.

At least they weren't flattering portraits. I tried to quell the nausea that the dictator's face evoked in me. What was this fixation about? In the beginning I had thought it was something akin to my own dread of suffering and war, the awe of hardship, but after today's description of the acid trip I realized that there was something else going on, something that I couldn't define but which I had to accept. There was a kind of hatred within Ken that was very similar to the evil in me . . . no, no, I wasn't ready to deal with that. I shuttled my precarious speculations back under cover, and praised these drawings as I had the others.

There was no doubt the boy had talent. He knew it, I admired it, and that, it seemed, was nice.

In fact, it made him insecure and me jealous, but neither of us would admit that yet.

"It must be nice to know what your career will be for the rest of your life," I mused wistfully.

"I suppose."

"Your parents must be awfully proud of you, aren't they?"

A wisp of a cloud passed between us.

"Actually," he said slowly, "my father still insists that it's a passing phase. He'd love to see me go, like my brother, to business school."

"I can't believe that! Not after seeing these. Wasn't he pleased when you won that five-hundred-dollar prize?"

"He said he was."

"Well, then?"

"He didn't mean it. He's rigid in his values, and besides, we've never connected. Ever since I was little we've had terrible fights over the slightest details. My mother used to say that it was because we're so much alike, but I can't see that. The thought that I could ever resemble him gives me the creeps."

"Doesn't that upset your mother?"

His mouth twisted unpleasantly. "It does. But that's just part of the parcel. I know you got a pretty poor impression of her downstairs, but that's not because of who she is; it's because of the situation around here. She's really a good person. She doesn't deserve the life she leads. It's stultifying! And she doesn't deserve me as a son or her marriage with my father, but that's the way it is, and there's nothing any of us can do about it, really. I hate to hurt her, but I can't help it." He swallowed hard and turned away from me. He was trapped in his situation the same way I was in mine. I understood, but was helpless. We stood, miles apart and at the same time touching, looking out the window into the damp, bleak afternoon. Glenridge kids, children of wealth and luxury. We had it all, and it made us sick. Deathly sick.

Trying to change the subject to brighten the scene, I asked, "Won't it help next year when you go off to college? By the way, what's the news from Yale? Have you heard anything?"

"Early acceptance."

"Ken! That's fantastic! Congratulations!" Another hold he had over me. In early December I'd finished my application to Yale, along with ones to Radcliffe and the University of Chicago. I expected them all to reject me. I was terrified that they would.

"It doesn't mean anything," he said glumly. "What's the difference?"

"Why do you put yourself down like that? I'd give anything to get early acceptance—or any acceptance. I'm sure they're going to reject me."

"I didn't know you applied there?" He looked happily surprised at the tidings. "Of course you'll get in. They just told me so quickly because I'd had my application in since September. Why do *you* put yourself down?"

"I guess it's part of the identity crisis," I laughed, using a too-easy out.

"Listen," he said, sliding the portfolios back under the bed. "I really am sorry for putting you through all my moods this afternoon. I guess maybe I'm not as together as I thought. But is there any hope that we could keep seeing each other every now and then?"

"Of course!" I lunged. Too eager. Cool it.

"Whew!" He grinned engagingly. "I keep thinking you're going to back down on me."

"Likewise, I'm sure. But I still don't understand why you want to be with me."

"Because you're beautiful, strong, smart, and compassionate. What do you see in me?"

"You sure don't have a very clear picture of me, but I won't correct it just yet. In you, however, I see the most talented, intelligent, sensitive person I've ever met. And I have a strong suspicion I'm in love with you." I looked him dead in the eye and tried to speak directly so it would not sound too thick or contrived.

He reached out to play with a strand of my hair. The sudden silence (Elton had long ago completed his serenade) overwhelmed me, and darkness was coming on. He put his hand behind my head, and pulled me toward him. I didn't protest. It was our first kiss since October, and it was awkward and uncertain, but I liked it. If all the future embraces were to be like this, I had nothing to fear.

"What do you think of him?" I demanded as my mother stirred the cream sauce for the chicken she and my father would eat tonight.

"He seems quite nice," she said distantly. There was a strain in her voice, and she refused to look at me when she spoke. I proceeded to cube the eggplant for a curry I was making for Ken and myself to eat.

"You don't like him, do you?" I should have let it drop, but as long as we'd gathered the nerve to have him for dinner, I wanted to know how it was going.

"It's too early for me to say whether I think he'd make my ideal son-in-law, if that's what you want. But he seems perfectly nice," she repeated. "But if I know you, it won't make any difference what I think, anyway." There was that familiar note of petulance and contrived hurt that she always orchestrated into the conversation when my father or I made decisions without first consulting her.

It should make me angry that she holds the reins so tightly, but I care too much. Instead, I feel guilty for upsetting her, and my eyes begin to water.

But now I am torn between allegiance to her and to my new leader, Ken.

"Why does everything have to be a struggle," I pleaded. "Why can't we just have a nice dinner, calm and normal. Not make a big deal over it?" My voice was barely audible. It sounded to me like a feeble whine.

"I'm not the one who's making a big deal. You're the one who's accusing me!" She fired the words like bullets across the kitchen.

"Please, Mom. Don't! I hate fighting so much." I buried my nose in a mountain of chopped vegetables.

She answered with a thunderous silence.

I put down my knife and slipped out to check on Ken's progress with my father. They sat rather formally across the living room from each other, but at least they were talking. Facts and figures, I suspected—my father's forte. It was hardly an animated conversation, more a stream of pauses and blurts. Still, there was an attempt at pleasantry.

Back in the kitchen, I found that my mother had fled to the back of the house. I tried to put the social dilemma out of my mind and turned my attention to cooking.

It was tricky to prepare food for both Ken and myself. I had to contrive ways to maintain my dietary restrictions and make him something that would taste substantial. We were both vegetarians, but he was not committed to losing weight as I was. Yet if I steamed the vegetables first with spices and diet sweetener, then I could separate them into portions and serve Ken's sprinkled with oil and chopped eggs. He would also have rice and, if he liked, bread. That should fill him up, I supposed, and no one would be the worse for my just eating spiced vegetables and water.

"Aimee, really!" My mother huffed back in. "Look at the mess you've made. Christ, I can't tell you how sick I am of this dual meal business. Why you can't eat like a normal human being I'll never know. We're going to have to wash every pot in the house!" This familiar quarrel was no pleasure trip, but I preferred it to discussion of Ken, at this point.

"Don't worry about it," I snarled. "I'll do the dishes. What difference does it make to you?" I washed the dishes every night, though not for the sake of appeasing her. I did it as a means of escaping from the table without seeming rude. I never had anything to contribute to the dinnertime conversation, but it would have unleashed unnecessary animosity if I were to vanish before my parents had finished coffee, so while they chatted or fought, I stood at the kitchen sink and played Cinderella. There was no way Mom could deny my argument, so she changed her tack.

"Whatever prompted Ken to get into this vegetarian kick?" she asked belligerently.

"He doesn't think we need to kill animals to keep ourselves alive."

"And just exactly why are you doing it?" She peered at me sharply. Odd that she chose this moment to ask me this question. I had, after all, been on this regimen for months. But she always timed her inquisitions to suit her moods.

So I tried to keep my reply even and calm. "Because I feel better for it."

She aggressively opened the oven door and began basting the chicken inside. "That's absurd, and you know it. Why don't you tell the truth? You're only doing this to cut calories, and you know it. Why do you play these ridiculous games?"

"Why do you care so goddamn much what I do?" I cried. "Why don't you get off my back! I'll eat what I want. It's my body, not yours. Why do you have to dwell on it so?" I was strangling on restrained sobs. Something had a hold on me from within, she had a hold on me from the outside, and I was being squeezed tighter and tighter between the two.

"Oh, for God's sake, calm down," she said disgustedly. "This was supposed to be a 'nice, calm, normal' dinner, wasn't it? Nobody's forcing you to eat anything you don't want to. I just think it's a shame. You looked so much prettier before you started to starve yourself."

"That's a matter of opinion," I retorted. "This stuff's done. Are you ready to eat?" I was anxious to get this meal over with.

Relations between my mother and Ken are strained from the beginning, for reasons I cannot fathom. He tries to be polite. He has nothing against her, and she won't specify what it is about him that she objects to. She calls him a "type," and mutters under her breath about drugs and sex. Nothing I say can allay her suspicions that Ken is corrupting her lily-white daughter. But she has no evidence to substantiate her accusations, so she just goes on assuming the worst. I wish she would quit second-guessing me and my actions.

"Nan, you don't have to tell me if you don't want to, but did you ever go to bed with Jed?"

"That's all right, it doesn't bother me to talk about something I never did. That's a funny question to fire at someone out of the blue, though. Why'd you ask?"

"Oh, I don't know. Sometimes I wonder if I'm weird to feel so disgusted by sex. You know, Ken and I have been together steadily now for over three months, and I still can't even imagine sleeping with him." The drone of a power mower filled Nan's kitchen. Her father was outside celebrating the rites of spring while, inside, we were preparing strawberry pies.

"Does he pressure you to go further than you want?"

"Oh, no, not at all. That's not even an issue between us. He knows how I feel about it, and is more than willing to hold off at least until we get to Yale next year. I suppose maybe my attitude will change if I get away from my parents . . . and at any rate I'm not about to do anything unless there's some sort of birth control."

"Do you think you *could* get pregnant? I mean, you're so tiny."

"You never know, and I'm not about to take any chances. God, what a waste that would be! Did you ever want to sleep with Jed?"

"I guess I was a little curious. Still am. But the whole thing scares me. It just seems like much more trouble and pain than it's worth. And besides, I know this sounds silly, but when Jed and I were together I felt so fat that I could never have taken my clothes off in front of him."

"You were never fat, Nan. What are you talking about?"

We were so much alike that it frightened me to listen. She now weighed less than I did, but still she called herself heavy, and fasted at least once a week. She brought her lunch to school in a bag every day, but would take a tiny bite of her sandwich and, complaining that she was full, then throw the rest away. She had far more discipline than I, and could spend hours in the kitchen without nibbling. I, alas, could not resist sneaking a berry from the pile we were hulling. Just as I put it in my mouth she turned and caught me. I felt like a thief and a glutton.

"You never were either!"

"What?" I asked, gulping the fruit.

"Fat!" she laughed. "Why are you looking so sheepish? You can have a strawberry if you want to!"

"Don't you ever eat when you cook? Strawberries have virtually no calories, you know." I felt obligated to decriminalize myself.

"I'm just not hungry. But you go ahead. We've got tons, more than enough for these pie shells. Have all you want."

Little did she know that, given my choice, I'd eat the whole three quarts. Faced with her lack of appetite, however, I managed to restrain myself and had no more.

"You're awfully lucky to be going to the same college as Ken, you know. Do you think you'll live together?"

The idea had never occurred to me.

"But we get assigned to roommates, don't we?" I was so naive. "Surely the authorities don't smile on boy-girl rooming."

"Oh, I don't know. My sister was living with a guy at U. Mass. and nobody up there said anything. Of course, she didn't tell my parents. I guess they just swapped rooms with people when they got there, or something. College is so loose, I think you could manage something if you wanted to. The question is, Would you want to live with Ken?"

"In most ways," I mused, "it would be the perfect arrangement. Frankly, I'm terrified of next year. There's going to be more than enough academic pressure, I should think, without a lot of social bullshit too. It might be neat if we could stay together—it would give me the perfect escape from a lot of strange guys. I mean, I'm sure I'll meet people on my own, and go to classes by myself, of course, but I honestly don't want another boyfriend besides Ken. It would make life much simpler if we did live together. . . . Aren't you afraid of going off all by yourself?"

"Terrified. I hear the University of Michigan's like a factory, too. To tell you the truth, I kind of expect to quit before the year is up. My parents have said I can come home if I decide I'm not cut out for it, and they won't be upset. It's just that I don't have any specific goals that require a college education, and I don't want to go out there and spend a lot of my parents' money so that I can flounder."

She looked exceptionally vulnerable this afternoon. Her jeans hung as loosely and bunched at the seat as badly as Kimmy's. And she wore her belt tightly cinched, which accentuated her gauntnesss.

"God, you've gotten skinny, Nan!"

"I'm not nearly as skinny as you," she flashed back defensively.

"Why, how much do you weigh now?"

"Ninety. How much do you?"

"The same. But you're at least two inches taller than I am."

"An inch doesn't make that much difference. It's bone structure that counts. You're much tinier than I am."

"The fact that you've got bigger bones than I do makes it all the worse for you to weigh so little, dummy."

"Christ, it's not a contest, Aimee! What are you getting so upset about?"

She was right, of course. Why was I getting so distraught? I could say that I was worried about her, but that would make a pretty flimsy excuse. The truth was, as she well knew, that it had become a contest between us, and I was chagrined that she was beating me so badly.

"I'm sorry. I think I'm actually jealous that you've been able to lose so much so fast. What is it, about thirty pounds since Christmas . . . five months?"

"Something like that," she murmured, and gingerly placed the pies in the oven. "Would you like to go for a walk? Down to the beach, maybe?"

"Love to. Always up for a walk."

She gave the counter a swipe with the sponge, dashed a bit of detergent on the dirty dishes in the sink, removed her apron, and led the way to the kitchen door.

"We're taking a walk down to the Point," she called up the back stairs to her mother. "Could you keep an eye on the pies for me? They should be done in a little less than an hour."

"Glad to, dear," her mother answered. Her voice was sweetly maternal, exactly fitting for Mrs. Cartman, who tended her family with the spritely air of a benevolent fairy. "Have a good time, but don't wear yourselves out!"

"My parents have been getting on my case for losing so much weight. They seem to think I'll collapse if I walk down the street. They've insisted that I go to the doctor tomorrow, because they worry I've ruined my precious body."

We took turns kicking a rock down the road a ways.

"You still have periods?" I asked.

"No. They stopped at the end of the first month. Which is fine by me. I hope they never start again."

"I know how you feel. My sentiments exactly."

"Have your parents hassled you much?"

"Naturally. But they keep sending me to the doctor, who runs me through all kinds of tests and proclaims me fit as a fiddle—why don't you gain a little weight, dear, he says, but otherwise says there's not a thing he can find wrong with me. So what can my parents do? Nobody can figure out what's going on with the periods, but they suspect one fine day they'll start of their own accord, and I'm in no rush!"

"Nobody's suggested therapy?"

"God, no! Why? There's nothing wrong with me psychologically. Have your parents suggested that, too?"

"Mm hmm. I have to go to a group therapy session on Thursday. It's so stupid. I'll go and listen, but I'm not going to open my mouth."

"I don't blame you. It's stupid. I mean, everybody around here is screwed up one way or another. There's nothing abnormal about us. In fact, I think we're a lot better off than nine-tenths of the people running around who control everything that's going on. You're probably much saner than the psychiatrists themselves. I mean, the experience will probably be interesting. There's a certain charm in the idea of going and having free license to spew out whatever you feel like. But you still have to keep your guard up, you know?"

Nan looked at me with an expression of relief. "Do you really believe that about our being stronger than they are? Do you think maybe they feel threatened by us, somehow?"

"Probably. Or at least, they're in awe of us. It sounds insane, but maybe it's something like celebrity. Everybody wants to be thin, after all. Right? Including the doctors, and our mothers, and our friends. We've achieved what they can't. They're jealous. They want to take it away from us."

"You think?"

"Well, I'm even jealous of you because you've taken it further than I can. Frankly, there's a part of me that wishes you'd never gotten into dieting. That's competition. But on the other hand, one of the reasons I feel close to you is that we understand each other that way. We have the same priorities in life."

"But my parents keep telling me they're worried—they're trying to help because they love me. Is that weird?"

Graduation Day. One of five hundred, I feel shrunken and lost. The sea of black-cloaked seniors tosses and churns with the catharsis of breaking and leaving. Proud parents cluster about, snapping pictures and crying maudlin tears. Mischievous undergrads hurl firecrackers into the bleachers where the graduates sit waiting to receive their diplomas, while overhead the sun flings its own rockets of scorching heat.

I yawn impatiently and try to distract myself by picking out the faces of family and friends in the crowd. There are my parents so gleefully proud, my father raising his camera, my mother reading to him from the program of events. I spy them and quickly look away. How dare they credit themselves with my success! I want to be proud, myself, of my acceptance by Yale, my honors grades and scholastic prizes, but am reminded always that I owe my fortune to them. Nothing I've achieved is legitimately mine. The hammer of guilt deals me its blow again and again, as harsh as the rays of this sun. Their eyes search for me, and I can almost hear their applause, my mother's raucous exclamations above the rest of the audience. But I won't take notice. A small act of defiance, but gratifying.

It's so contrived, this ceremonial hoopla. We swelter in these shroudlike gowns. We look like fools in these tasseled caps. We smirk and ridicule each other. And all for the sake of the parents. There are those among my classmates who seem to enjoy themselves, however. What is wrong with me?

Our stands are constructed in a horseshoe. We have been placed alphabetically by last name, so Nan and Ken sit across from me. Their faces wear the same exasperation as mine, I'm relieved to see. But Nan, so frail these days, looks as though she's ready to pass out. I'm sorry that she's done this to herself, sorry that because of it our friendship has ripped apart at last. Because of her weakness, or mine? That she has taken discipline so far that it has become a sickness she cannot stop, or that I haven't the discipline to keep up with her? A combination of the two, I think, has damned us, broken us apart forever, just as a similar combination prevented Kim from ever becoming the best friend I wished her to be as a child. She too sits across from me now, wraithlike and miserable, her ghostly eyes staring vacantly toward the speaker's podium.

The headmaster has begun calling names. In the midst of the others I notice Candy's, and start. I didn't realize that she was still here. Rumor had it that she'd been hospitalized already. Too weak to walk. But no, there she is. Barely there. I whisper to Dee sitting next to me, and learn that she's been released on the condition that she gain ten pounds by the end of the month. And will she go to college? Probably not, Dee grimly whispers back.

Then we are beckoned to rise and shine and fly into the future. Our future. I march in one direction. Ken with his diploma already in hand passes in the other. He smiles, blows me a kiss, and moves ahead.

And suddenly, it's over. False congratulations, undeserved awards, fraudulent glory, and all. We shake hands, wish each other luck, and hail the miracle of our coming of age.

Chapter Six

Less Becomes More

YALE COLLEGE WELCOMES the class of '75! As the carillons of Harkness Tower chime out one greeting and the blazing September sun beats down another, fifteen hundred excited freshmen flood the gates of the Old Campus. They trample the freshly manicured lawns, invade the Yale Coop, and take Durfee Sweet Shoppe by storm. For most this is their first major step away from home, and they leap at it like impatient puppies straining at the bit. While their parents tag along behind, lugging boxes and bellowing pride in their Ivy League offspring, the young men and women hurl themselves into the project of dormitory homemaking. Brawny boys, their backs drenched with late summer sweat, heave sofas in and out of entryways. Girls, enthusiastic pioneers in cutoffs and halter tops, attack Vanderbilt Hall. Armed with buckets, disinfectant, and mops, they're prepared to do battle with the telltale traces of their masculine predecessors and establish a style of their own. Everywhere you look there's something happening, people laughing, and change brewing. I can't believe I'm a part of this scene.

But, yes. It's true. I'm a legitimate member of the Yale community, and I belong here every bit as much as the others. We're all strangers here, all refugees from childhoods good and bad. But we have more in common than just that. We've all as well accepted the challenge of academic excellence and a certain kind of snob appeal. The only difference between them and me is that I can't go it alone. I want to. I tear myself away from my parents with a vicious exuberance and swear that Glenridge will never again be my home. But when it comes down to facing forward and marching into the unknown, I freeze. While my new classmates clamor and meet, tossing Frisbees around the courtyard and comparing notes of origin, I scan the crowds for Ken and gravitate toward him like a homing pigeon. He'll help me through the rough spots ahead, I assure myself. He'll get me through and be my man.

I never worry that Ken might not be as anxious to live together as I am. We did, after all, spend the entire summer dreaming up strategies for the coming year. They were fantasies then, but now that the semester's begun we move like conspirators to realize the schemes. First he convinces the Silliman dean that he needs a single room for the sake of his artwork. The ploy works, and the dean finds an empty suite at the top of the Silliman Tower, six flights up, where we can live in privacy. "What a great way to keep in shape," I pant, glowing with the triumph. The suite is enormous, airy, and light. We have three rooms to ourselves, a wide, functioning fireplace, and a view that spans Silliman courtyard and continues to the sea beyond. We scour college attics for ownerless furniture, and scavenge two lamps, a mattress, and chairs. In a couple of days our residence is intact, and we settle down to play house.

The setup seems too good to be true. Ken and I are like children together, intimate pals unwilling to let each other out of sight. We attend classes together, taking literature for my sake and art for his and a host of extraneous courses to satisfy distributional requirements. We study side by side at the library, read one another to sleep at night, and exchange moral support whenever the academic going gets rough. Three times a day we troop to the dining hall for our version of meals. Eating vegetarian on institutional cooking is never an easy task, but Yale at least offers daily salads, fruit, and cheese. We manage to maintain our spartan regimen, and I for the first time in years eat regularly without suffering anger or guilt on account of it. There are no dinnertime flare-ups over excess calories, no concerned proddings to supplement my diet with bread and meat. I can take as much or as little as I want of whatever I please. Ken and I accept each other's epicurean eccentricities as part of our mutual accord, and so, as I pile my plate high with rabbit food and he mixes gruesome concoctions of peanut butter and jam, neither of us says a word. It is an adjustment for me to do all of my eating in public, of course, no matter how understanding Ken tries to be. No more secret binges, no kitchen to raid, no more culinary sabotage and, with Ken's constant companionship, no opportunity for purgative measures. I do not, however, feel deprived. Our new joint ritual is much more satisfying than my crazy old games. Always alone, always at a table for two, we secure a comfortable bubble of silence around us and observe as the rest of the Yale community stages its show. I enjoy the hubbub well enough, but feel no temptation to desert my companion and go join in. We cling together like magnets, attending movies, concerts, lectures, and plays. On weekends we drop into and out of parties and mixers, always as spectators, never taking part. Oblivious to our reputation as social freaks, we smile proudly on learning that others refer to us as KenandAimee and consider us the Siamese twins of the freshman class. Mockery or not, we take comfort in our arrangement and, by mutual consent, allow it to preclude individual freedom.

So it's a compromise, we tell each other. And the primary bargain we have to strike concerns sex. I put it off as long as I can by pleading fear of pregnancy, though I'm well aware that my body's about as fertile as a four-year-old child's (it's now four years since my last period). Ken understands. He agrees with my hesitancy and is willing to wait. But not forever. Finally, hiding my reluctance, I make an appointment to see the university gynecologist, and breathe a sigh of relief when informed that the waiting list is three months long. "Nothing to do but wait," I inform Ken, and turn up my nose when he suggests intermediary measures. "I'd rather wait than spoil it, don't you think?" He shrugs disappointedly, and nods. So, in the meantime, we sleep together in innocence, I wearing my pale pink gown, he in his boxer shorts. We restrict our lovemaking to tender caresses, kisses and hugs, and I can't imagine why Ken minds. His desires elude me because I have none. Passion, to my mind, exists only in literature—physical passion, that is to say—and intercourse amounts to rape.

At last, however, my stall is up. In the middle of November I'm granted an appointment at D.U.H., and fitted for a diaphragm. Grudgingly, I take my stash of equipment and foam, and return to my loyal partner. He thinks I'm just as excited as he, and I do my best to keep up the show. Ken's still my idol, no matter how I loathe this business. It isn't his fault that he has these obnoxious desires, I tell myself. For him, they're natural. And it can't do me any harm. It's not that I have any moral objections to this trial, it's simply a matter of taste. But now, when we meet, naked and hesitant at the end of the day, all I can ever think of is getting it done with. Those first two months of sleeping together were nothing like this. I submit, as I suppose I am supposed to, and lie down to let him take over. We fumble, and laugh nervously. He makes me feel fat and embarrassed as he runs his fingers along my ribs, caresses my shoulders, and kisses me. His touch is so gentle, so loving and tentative. Why, then, does it make me cringe? I break out in gooseflesh as he fondles me, lie rigid and cold as he strokes my belly and thighs. Please, just get this over with, I want to scream, but instead I suffer in silence, and try to respond to his touch. Visions of the attic where Cliff and Dick played horse with me, images of Tony and his Saran wrap ploy, and of the make-out session with Billy and Stan keep my mind occupied as Ken comes down. And still I can't understand why I hate this so. Oh, God, just finish, and leave me alone! But it seems interminable, a gross, humiliating endurance test. He looms over me in the dark, a monster who plunges and sways, then descends and stabs at the dry, tight-barreled well beneath him. I grit my teeth and moan as if with pleasure, and finally he drops, clutching and kissing and exhausted. We whisper how much we love each other, I hating him for his gross insensitivity. And then he sleeps.

One morning in early winter we rise as usual at eight and stand in the bathroom side by side. I wear a long woolly bathrobe, snow white and soft as a lamb. He's clothed only in a towel. We take our customary poses and perform our matutinal rituals, but there's a difference from previous mornings. It's a difference in my perception only, and for no apparent reason, but when I look over at him hunched above the washbasin next to me, I'm horrified. He looks to me this morning like an ugly little man/boy, a stranger, a troll. He's too everything at once—too old, too immature, too short, too pale. The sight of his naked body offends me, not in an emotional way, but—for the first time I admit it—aesthetically. His hair is kinky, straggling, and thinning, and all of a sudden the thought of spending any more of my life with Ken strikes me as pure insanity.

We're totally out of synch. He tries to tell a joke between shaving and brushing his teeth, and I can't even fake a laugh. He's offended, asks why I'm so on edge. I snap back, insisting it's nothing, that it has only to do with me. And so, really, it has. I am, for the first time, glimpsing my own strength and will, by contrast with him. It's a mean way to come into my own, but there it is and I can't deny it. Before he catches the expression of astonishment that's pouring across my face, I turn and scurry back to the bedroom, half hoping this revelation will fade away. But the sensation grows stronger by the instant, and when he appears in the bedroom doorway I plead ill and urge him to go on down to breakfast without me. He throws me a baffled look, more worried than suspicious, and asks if I'm going to be all right. "It's just my stomach," I try to assure him. "It'll probably pass in a few minutes. You go ahead. I'll meet you at the library later."

When he finally leaves, I prop my feet up on the window ledge, and stare out across the courtyard. The smell of bacon wafting up from the Silliman kitchen teases me. I wonder what it would be like to go into the dining hall alone. To pass by Mary at the identification desk, and pick up my tray, go through the line, and choose a table by myself, or with someone other than Ken. Every day, three times a day for four months, we've been together constantly, and it's been great and it's all been, for the most part, my doing. Then, what's so different now, all of a sudden? What's so different is that at last I'm coming together. And it's about time. This isn't precocity, the frustration of pushing forward and holding back at the same time; this is finally my chance to go do it on my own. And I'm blowing the whole deal by clutching at Ken. It's not really that I love him. No, to face the facts, I've been deluding myself on that score. It's just that I haven't had the courage to tackle alone the challenges of life, of college, of men.

But, though disappointed with my relations with Ken, I keep wondering about sex. Sex as it should, and maybe could be on someone else's, on my own terms. I need to explore. It won't be any different with someone else, warns that ugly inner voice of reckoning. You're the one who's weird on that score, not Ken. You're the one who's frigid. You've never wanted sex. You've done your best to make yourself unattractive to men, and you've used this little-girl look to seduce them in other ways, to make them want to take care of you, to abide by your rules of the game. Because, at the same time that you're deadly afraid of the threat, you crave the attention and affection that other people get with sex. You want romance without passion, is what it boils down to, and that is just not natural. Nor is it fair to either side. You use your looks and your helpless wiles to seduce them emotionally, but then you pull a number when it comes to bed. You turn off, move by rote, and numb yourself to the pleasure and, yes, to the pain as well. You feel nothing except insult at the violation, and you convince yourself that you haven't asked for it. But you're your own kind of tease, let's face it. You're no different from Kimmy at the end of high school, when she broke with her boyfriend and got so thin. She flirted like a 42d Street whore, though she spouted rage if any of her suitors tried to press her to love. It was as though she expected her emaciation to act as a natural shield against sex, and a release from all social responsibility. She'd crook her finger and the boys would come running, and she'd tease along until she got tired, then expect them all to fade away. She was honestly horrified when accused of leading them on, and would protest the accusations by showing off her wraithlike body and turn the table against her suitors by telling them they were crazy to bother with anyone so nonsexy. It was a horrid dance to watch, but worse yet to find yourself doing it, as you have with Ken. And it's all because you haven't the guts to stand up for yourself. You expect him to shoulder the burden of your dreams and help you through the rough spots, but you still can't trust him in return. Well, you can't let yourself get away with that any longer, and it's not fair to anybody to keep on trying to. It's true, besides, what Mom's been saying ever since she found out about the rooming arrangement, that you're cutting yourself short by coming to Yale and immediately shacking up with your high school boyfriend. Who's kidding whom, with all this talk about love and devotion? She sees through it, and so now do you. You've been damning her whenever she calls and tries to rout you out. You say she's trying to screw you up, but take an objective look at things, and you see that she's acting in your behalf. She's trying to push you ahead, not pull you down. It isn't Ken she objects to, really, but the closure of the relationship that you yourself have engineered. You're the one, much more than Ken. You're dragging him and yourself right down the drain.

Oh, of course he goes along with it all. You haven't given him a minute to give it a second thought. And he's going to be lost when you leave him. You've made sure that he clings to you every bit as much as you to him, only now that you don't want to cling any longer you're faced with the consequences. Though suddenly you can't stand the sight of him, how do you expect him to relinquish his grip. He's not going to feel the same way. He's going to protest, to make scenes, and there's going to be a terrible temptation for you to feel sorry for him and stand by. But you can't. This morning was just the beginning. You saw him as a weak, nervous little person whom you could no longer connect with, and that view of him is not simply going to go away. If you pull yourself together and snap the cords right away, maybe you can hang on to the healthy part of the relationship and keep in touch with him through the upcoming changes, but if there's any delay he's going to become your new monster. For his sake and yours, you have to make the break quickly and cleanly, and soon.

It's not really so surprising, if you think about it. Ever since that first day in the library you've found fault with him. Sure, they were minor, silly objections, and they were obscured by the magnetic draw he had on you, but they haven't lessened or gone away, even so. And now that you're changing and strengthening, those stupid criticisms are becoming important. They're exploding. You had him pegged as a hero to worship and serve, but he's no hero, and you can't delude yourself on that score any longer. You have to be your own hero from now on. Oh, he's gentle and kind, and he probably genuinely loves you, but he can't live your life for you. Sure, you thought that through him you could avoid all the hard parts of growing up. That was the initial attraction, right there. All that bit about drugs and obsession and abstinence and endurance, all the enigmas that you couldn't juggle on your own you foisted off on him, and he accepted the burden. You could listen and watch him perform the feats that you couldn't, and because he survived you took him as your idol. You were terrified, fragile, confused; you had in effect suspended your growth. But now that you're coming out of that spell, you've got to get away from him and explore on your own. He's been your surrogate long enough. This isn't love, it's cowardice. If it were love you wouldn't lie and suffocate him so, and if he really loved you in a positive way, he wouldn't surrender to your clutch. It's not healthy.

Health! It's beginning to dawn on me that that's the root of the problem. I stand up and walk across the room to confront my newest mirror image. We have no curtains on the windows, and the cold December light illuminates me with pure, revealing clarity. I look tired, but proud, and strong in a way I've never noticed before. My eyes gleam darkly, and my cheeks are soft and smooth. Though still not exactly heavy, I feel a certain weight to myself, and it feels good. My body has a little flesh to grab, and the bones show less glaringly. I don't mind the difference. I enjoy the sense of muscle. It somehow certifies my rights as a human being. What's the point of killing yourself to be so thin and ethereal, when the fact of the matter is, you're a physical creature? It's all part of the self-delusion, the sham. What was it that Carol said? "I like myself too much to hurt my body that way." Body and self, one and the same. How, why, have I tried so hard to separate the two? Love without sex, appetite without eating, performance without reward, devotion without respect. It's all part of the same terrible, pointless war I've been waging these years, and it's got to end, starting now. It doesn't make sense to go on hurting myself, or the others around me. It all has to change, to become part of a whole picture instead of a shattered one. I can't stay a confused little girl forever.

I walk back to the window, open it, and poke my head

outside. The rush of cold air brings a flush to my skin. My eyes sting at the blast and my hair whips back from my face. Far below, the rush to early morning classes has begun. I know the people passing only by sight. There goes that skinny little Texan girl who eats her toast with knife and fork. And the guy who makes a sport of carrying stacks of filled coffee cups across the dining hall. Yesterday he managed a record eight without spilling a drop, and the whole place broke into applause. But I don't even know his name. A few straggling couples walk arm in arm to the gate, then part, heading off in separate directions, and the master's kids have come out to play tag with their dog and Rami, the Indian student who lives downstairs. The morning is quiet yet, since most Yalies sleep late and orient their schedules around afternoon classes, but there's something soothing and inspiring about these early hours. It's too beautiful to ignore.

Quickly, I pull on my jeans, an old shirt of my brother's, and a big woolly sweater, and run downstairs. I take the steps two at a time. It's ridiculous how I've cloistered myself! I want to tour the campus, to see it for the first time on my own. Outside the entryway looms Woolsey Hall, where Ken and I just last week saw a Miles Davis concert. But it looks strange now, an edifice I've never really seen before. It's monumental in scale, and rather ugly, but nice, comforting, like an old weathered giant who guards the years. These past months I've come by it six, seven times a day, but just now I'm looking at it for the first time. What is this? It's a matter of perception, a changing point of view.

Chas Everett, a tall blond who lives on Rami's floor, comes up behind me. He has a jelly doughnut in one hand, a stack of books in the other. A soft, moonstone blue sweater is casually slung around his neck, and his shirt, obviously donned in haste, billows loose about his long lean body. He has hair the color of white sand, and shocking blue eyes. He's so good-looking! How can I never have seen him before? He tosses me a look of surprise. Am I staring? No, it's just that he's never seen me alone like this. I muster my confidence and say hello. He smiles, bemused, and returns the greeting, then hurries on to class.

It's after nine now, and Cross Campus is deserted. The sun's just breaking through the morning mist, shining slyly over the top of Sterling Tower and lighting up the statue above, the Archangel Gabriel blowing his horn. What is this curious feeling of elation and freedom? I've never noticed these details before, never known this pure delight in just looking and standing still. I needn't move, or leap, or talk. It's a pleasure just staying, alone.

A chilly gust of wind cuts across College Street, stabbing me to the bone. I wrap my sweater tightly about me, sliding my hands up the sleeves. I'm sick of being so cold all the time. What's the difference whether I'm skinny or not; I'd rather be healthy and warm. Yes, it's dawning on me what a foolish life I've been leading, unnatural and sick. And for what? No one cares, really, about that. About the obsessions and the false intensity, about my contrived substitutions for life. No, no one else cares, and neither, any longer, do I. All this time I've refused, adamantly, to expose myself, to tell the truth, but now the jig is up. The subterfuges aren't enough anymore. Modeling, dieting, Ken, exercise, all of it was just one great evasion. I didn't have the nerve ever to show how I honestly felt, what I thought, what I wanted. What a joke! Ken had it nailed right at the start when he called me aloof. I should have taken the clue back then, but instead I ducked further into my fear tactics, letting everybody go on thinking I had my act together, that I knew exactly what I wanted and how to get it. Sure, I was so positive, self-motivated, conscientious, pretty, and bright. It was one steady stream of perfection, my notoriety. Everything to the nth degree, and I never let on the truth. Not to anyone. Not to my parents, not to Ken. Not to myself.

A sprightly rendition of "The Times They Are A-Changin'" peals out from Harkness Tower. The carillon players are practicing early today. The music slices through the morning silence, lifting my spirits and propelling me forward. I'm going to have to confront Ken, and tell him what's happening.

"But I can't understand where this is coming from," he protested. "Is it sex, or what? I mean, if that's blowing your mind somehow, let's change, do something different. We can go easier."

"It has nothing to do with sex," I insisted, averting my eyes from his searing stare. "I just think we're making a mistake."

"You've been talking to your mother again," he accused petulantly. "You can't handle being torn between her and me. You do realize, don't you, that a week ago you were suggesting marriage." His voice was hard, frozen, and he toyed with his knife as he spoke. The sounds of lunch roared a serenade.

It was true that my mother and Ken had been ripping me in opposite directions so hard that I had proposed. It might make life easier if our connection were legal. Now I shuddered at the thought.

"No," I vowed, "that suggestion was just a lunatic idea, a last desperate—well, a mistake, obviously. I guess it was so extreme that it prompted me to start reevaluating what we're doing to ourselves. It has nothing to do with Mom. I'm ready to break from her the same as from you. The time has come for me to grow up, Ken. I can't keep gripping other people for

Less Becomes More   203

shelter all my life. Can you understand that it has nothing, per se, to do with you? It's just not a good idea to stick together like this anymore."

"It wasn't entirely my idea to live together," he muttered.

"No. And I'm not accusing you. I take all the blame, okay? I admit that I've behaved like an imbecile, a spoiled brat, really. It is my fault, and I'm sorry that I didn't realize before this happened. It's screwed us up, and I know it, and I'm sorry." I watched the steam from my coffee rise, curl, and dissipate.

"But why? Why has it?" he pleaded. I couldn't believe how weak he sounded, weak and little-boyish. He and I have kept each other from growing up, I realized, astonished. This was the king of my fantasies! My God! He looked at me with wide, moony eyes, like those of a puppy begging to be petted. "Even if you move out, we can still be together, can't we? I don't see why this has to be the end of the relationship, or why you even want it to be."

I struggled with the answer now, for I had thought myself that we could continue to see each other, but the closer we came to the end, the more I saw that the cut had to be final and complete. Not knowing where the explanation was coming from, I began. "I'm afraid you've sort of been my victim, Ken. The same way I've been my own victim." He looked totally confused, and I stumbled on. "It has to do with courage and freedom. It's not easy to grow up and be by yourself. That's why neither of us has done it. That's why we've kept each other from going ahead, or at least why I've used you to keep myself from moving. But I can't keep using people and habits and appearances as shields to protect myself from challenge. I mean, I never let myself see what I was doing, any more than I let you or my parents see it, but it's like I've always had to have some distraction to keep myself from facing forward, some excuse to take the fear out of expectation." He was watching me as though I were mad, but I ignored him and kept on going. "You see, I knew innately that I could become someone vital and strong, in any one of a number of directions. You know what I mean. It's the same with any of us in Glenridge. The world of the privileged, right? Everything at our fingertips. Doctor, lawyer, Indian chief, we can be what we want to be, do what we want to do. But how in hell are we supposed to figure out what that is? Here I go, the spoiled brat talking again, but it was precisely that fear of choosing that's made me cop out the way I have. Yeah, cop out. I've dwelt on myself so much that it's downright boring. My body, my dreams, my mind, my face. It's disgusting. The only thing I haven't let myself confront is my life, the most important thing."

"Now wait a minute," Ken broke in. "What makes you so different from any of the rest of us? You're giving yourself an awful lot of credit for sensitivity, aren't you?"

"No. I'm just glad that I've come to my senses at last, late though it may be. It's still not too late. I guess everybody has his or her time of behaving like a baby, but I've overextended mine, and I realize it, and I'm sorry. What more do you want me to do? I wish you weren't involved, because I really don't think you quite understand what's been going on, and I can't adequately explain it to you. I wish I'd had the nerve to try drugs, or become some kind of rebel. If I had it might have snapped me awake sooner, but I was too much of a good girl, or just too cowardly to do that. Instead I twisted myself all around and sucked you in in the bargain. It was all part of the great escape."

"That's absurd." His voice was hollow.

"It may sound absurd to you, but it's true. You were just as much an evasion for me as everything else. And a compulsion. You haunted me because, at least in my mind"—I was trying to keep the blame on myself, not to implicate or condemn Ken—"you mirrored a lot of my self-doubts and concerns. I mean, you can't deny that we found a lot in common."

"That's normally considered the basis for love and understanding," he remarked cynically, and made a stabbing gesture at his untouched grilled cheese sandwich.

"Ken, can't you see how sick this relationship is? I don't know why, I honestly don't, but this morning it hit me like a bulldozer. The way we're living, doting, depending on each other for every bit of life. God, we're practically sucking each other's blood. Before you came along I blinded myself to the world around me by dwelling on food, modeling, my weight, anything profoundly superficial. And now I'm blinding myself by living through you—which is not to say," I added hastily, "that you're superficial, but our relationship is. Oh, Christ, people are weird. I'm weird. It all sounds zany, and I do feel cruel, but I really believe what I'm saying. I've involved you in a chain of deathly obsessions, and if it goes on it's going to hurt us both. Look, just look at what it's done to you!"

In fact, he looked horrified and panicky. He twitched and wiggled in his seat, and his mouth quivered as though he might cry. It felt cruel to run him through the wringer like this, but when I'd started I had no idea just how warped our relationship had become, and how vulnerable he was. He didn't remove his gaze from my face, but stared hungrily, pleadingly, as though by relaying distress signals he might win me back. But the process was irreversible now. Something that could never be recaptured was over.

"It's like a disease, this whole thing," I tried valiantly to convince him. The discussion was making me feel frighteningly powerful and strong. The strength wasn't very pretty, but it was real, and it surged forth like a geyser now after being bottled up for years. All the power I'd never found to tell the truth, to stand up for myself. It all came welling out at Ken. It was wicked, almost demonic, but I couldn't help it. I knew that, in the long run, it was to his benefit as well as mine. "Look, we've been doing this Bobbsey Twins routine for months, pretending that it makes us happy, but how can something that's as stifling as this make anyone happy?"

"I never heard you complain before," he said lamely.

"No, never. And that's exactly what was wrong. Like I say, I don't know what's hit me now, but I'm beginning to realize that I don't even know the definition of happiness. I mean I have absolutely nothing to compare this with. I've made you my first, last, and only lover, and that's sheer madness."

"You're selling me kind of short, aren't you?"

"Jesus Christ! I don't mean that I regret the past few months. We've created our own little version of paradise, if you want to get cute about it. And I do love you. But this can't go on. It's destroying us both. We've got to get out of this rut, meet other people, take risks, and test ourselves in a real way instead of settling into this fantasy existence. It probably seems to you that I'm being really selfish, and maybe I am, but it wouldn't do you any good to hang on with me feeling like this. I should have woken up years ago, but I didn't. There's a time when you have to let go, and that time unfortunately is now."

He looked so bleak I wanted to put my arms around him and tell him that it would be all right. It would be, even though or perhaps because we would never be together again. But I didn't do that. I just sat on my side of the table and watched the silent tears slide down his cheeks. I felt helpless and sad, but there was nothing for it. My strength was yet too

Less Becomes More   207

tentative for me to risk it with sorrow or regret. So instead I waited and watched, and with every passing second my conviction in breaking up increased.

At last the tears subsided. He pulled himself together, and, without saying a word, fled the dining hall. That afternoon I packed my belongings, left him alone in the tower suite, and moved to the room and roommates I'd been officially assigned at the beginning of the year.

Once the initial exhilaration began to pall, there were moments of loneliness and insecurity when I wanted to run back to Ken, but I restrained myself. My decision was a sound one, and I knew it. Too long I had made a practice of dividing myself into conflicting parts, of making a scapegoat of either body or mind, of setting up agonizing battles between my actions and my dreams. I had prided myself on reversing my instinctual appetites, and now, for the first time, I dared myself to let go.

Not surprisingly, I began to hang out in the dining halls, the social centers of the campus. I did not, as I had so long feared, lose control and eat myself to oblivion. Nor did I make a fool of myself when faced with strangers. Though hesitant and awkward at first, I forced myself to join groups of people, to introduce myself, and participate in discussions. It astonished me to discover that I was welcome. My new friends joked about my vegetarian salads and my peculiar eating habits, but the teasing was good-natured, and the communal atmosphere forbade me to take offense. I began to loosen my dietary restrictions even further than I had through Ken, to eat bread and cheese and, occasionally, fish, and my weight climbed over one hundred for the first time in five years. The resulting power surprised me. This was no longer stamina, but was actual muscular and emotional strength. I was turning into a fully functioning adult, a woman.

I learned that my classmates considered me beautiful and desirable, which presented me with a new range of apprehensions, partly because it was such an unexpected development, and partly because I myself was interested in a number of men. Toward the end of freshman year my periods started up again, sporadically at first, then perfectly regular, and with this change my body filled out, just as it had at age twelve. Only this time I gave in and accepted it. I had better things to do now than to attempt to hold back the clock. And one of those things was to explore the world of men, to embark, if you will, on my own sexual holiday. Of course, it was tentative at first. I drilled my new roommates for their perspectives on sex. What was so appealing about it? What's in it for the woman? Is it duty or fun? We held long hesitating talks about female orgasm and the emotional role of sex, and they assured me that there were times when it was just as enjoyable for the woman as for the man. This initially was hard for me to believe, but they, considerably more experienced than I, kept urging me to experiment, trust, and risk occasional disappointments. It will be worth the trouble in the long run, they promised. So I began to take up some of the offers I was receiving, and slowly, haltingly, became acquainted with my own femininity. It did, eventually, prove to be worth the trouble.

What was fascinating was the speed and extent to which my body changed. It was as though my hormones wanted to make up for lost time. Hips, bust, waist—in a matter of months I resembled the proverbial hourglass. "Where did this come from?" my friends would laugh, and all I could do was shrug helplessly. I still couldn't stand the sight of the curves and the feel of the new softness, but I had better things to do than agonize over it.

When I came home for vacation at the end of freshman year I found two strangers waiting to greet me. There was a strikingly beautiful woman and a gentle, handsome man—two people I had never seen before. Sensitive, funny, intelligent, and kind, my parents were, I realized for the first time, incredible individuals, and I was downright lucky to be their daughter. How could I so long have squirmed under the fortune of my home? Their successes were no threat to me! That notion was a product of my own nightmare. They had never been out to dictate my course, to force or block me into directions I didn't want to take. Their concern for me was founded on love, not criticism, and was intended not to control but to help me choose what I wanted from life. Our shared attitudes, character traits, and physical qualities were just trimmings on the package whose content, they'd been trying to tell me all these years, depended on my own designs. Now that at last I had found the courage to explore these designs, they were ready to stand back and applaud.

I began to realize how totally I'd distorted the truth about my family as I was growing up. My parents were avidly in love with each other, always had been, and they adored both my brother and me! I flinched at the thought of all the mistaken pain I'd imposed on myself as a child, of the disasters I'd imagined would break the family apart. Volatility was a natural ingredient in my parents' relationship, not a signal of its dissolve. These people admired and respected each other, just as they did me. Human emotions, disagreement, and conflict were just part of the bargain. It was a shame that it took me so long to appreciate that, but now that I could see clearly it was like having double vision. Objectively speaking, the domestic scene was the same as ever. The willful silences and shrill cries of frustration rang out now as they had when I was twelve. The only difference lay in my perception of the truth and my willingness to probe beyond appearances. Just as I couldn't find out who I would become by studying my reflection in the looking glass, so I couldn't learn my family's secrets by searching its veneer. No, some things must be left unsaid, sensed without reason, and trusted instead of forced. There are times when you just have to leap on faith, and know that you'll land safe and sound.

After the Fast: A Postscript

So, looking back over the troubled years, I ask myself . . . what happened? What prompted me to such inane obsessions, and what exactly sparked me out of them? How could I and so many of my friends hate ourselves the way we did? I wonder if we were so different, really, from any "normal," confused adolescents. Had we had the courage, would we have opted for drugs, alcohol, or more overt rebellion to answer the same fears that ate at us from the inside?

The pieces of the puzzle spin wildly about me even now. No analyst, no expert, I can only conjecture through retrospect. Perhaps if I had risked exposing my underlying emotions, and my parents had realized and allowed for a contrast between their and my perceptions of our life together, perhaps if we had all worked to overcome the communications barriers, the breakthrough could have started earlier. But as it was, I had to leave home before my shell could start cracking. Then, even as

I clung to Ken, my vestige of protection, the lures of freedom and adventure began to get through to me. Though I tried to maintain my image of dependency and immaturity and pretended to bask in the cowardly comforts of our tight relationship, the magnetic draw of college life refused to let me delude myself. Ken was not my hero, and I no longer wanted to hide within my little-girl role, but for those first few months I blinded myself to the feelings of unrest by wallowing in our mutual commitment. I was like a spring, winding tighter and tighter until at last I broke and, jerking wildly, knocked over all the untidy sentiments in my path.

The gravest casualty of this unleashing, of course, was Ken. For his love was the fuel that brought me to my turning point. That moment of dread as I stood at the washbasin arose out of the realization that I had asked him to marry me. It was the slow horror that I had begged for entrapment and that my passion for self-denial was on the verge of destroying both our lives. Marriage negated every dream I'd ever cherished for a future life, and yet I'd proposed so glibly, almost unconsciously! The move was the last in a long series of desperate attempts to rebel, to draw attention to myself, and in an inverse way to assert control. But this time I was not my only victim, and as I watched Ken mutely grappling, gradually succumbing to my will, I recoiled in disgust. It was a twofold revulsion both for my own misguided demands and for the sickening weakness I could see through Ken in myself. That weakness was a quality we shared. We liked to call it sensitivity, but I saw clearly now that it was blatant insecurity. And just as clearly I saw that our mirroring of each other, which had solaced us at the start, was beginning to destroy us. I had so fastidiously been tightening the net, however, that it was almost impossible to back out. The only way was to cut and run.

Better late than never, so the saying goes, and I believe it. The thrill of exploring life with abandon, not insanely but freely, is worth struggling for, even if it means bruising those who stand in the way. For the push, the conflict, and the pain are all part of the bargain of feeling alive. It isn't always easy or pleasant to stand alone, laugh at yourself, and let the world come close enough to touch, but it's far more rewarding than shutting yourself away like a dressed-up doll under a crystal bell.

My parents ask me now if they were to blame for my early craziness, and I wonder that they can even think it could be one side's fault. They couldn't see past my facade any better than I could see past theirs, it's true, but is blindness a crime? Paling at every shiver of turbulence I ran in one direction; appalled at my obsessions they ran in the other. We were respecting each other's right to privacy and were trying to balance the boat. How could we know how close we came to sinking? We would have had to risk shattering those facades which seemed so agreeable, but we might then have seen the truth. The truth was that those years, like it or not, were a painful time, a time when the highs were higher and the lows lower than they ever had been before, and perhaps ever would be after. It was a time when the line between growth and casualty was at its frailest, when nothing could be taken for granted, and nothing came easily or for free. My fortune was that I walked the line without falling, without it breaking, and that once I reached the other side I felt no urge to go back. My friends and I were the lucky survivors.

Of those in our skinny club some, like Candy, grew out of their fears and distractions by falling in love. I was one of those who reversed the process, discovering independence only after shedding the illusion of love. Kimmy began to regain her health during a trip to Europe with a close circle of friends, Nan after quitting college, when she moved up to New Hampshire and joined a commune. It took individual courage, along with support from family and friends, but eventually we all learned that distraction is no ticket to life, and that exploring the world as young women is far more exhilarating than remaining perennial little girls.

And yet it's too easy to sit back now and say calmly that the breakthrough comes automatically as a result of time. I regret having dampened with morbid obsession what could 'ave been joyous and fruitful years. But there is no formula for easing the pain of growing up. The lesson that life, though never simple, has a lot to give is one that everyone must learn in his or her own way. Where, how, and with whom each individual spends that life creates a unique fretwork that changes shape at every stage of the game. No single force, not parent, teacher, friend, or even oneself, can take the blame or glory for the ultimate form that results. The best we can hope to do for each other is to recognize the rough spots and, as we stumble through them, work together to smooth the way.